Margaret H. Roda
Turnhouse

PING
WOMEN'S GOLF YEAR
92-93

· EDITED BY NICK EDMUND ·

WITH A
FOREWORD BY
MICKEY WALKER

First Edition

KENSINGTON WEST
PRODUCTIONS

First published 1993

© Nick Edmund 1993

Nick Edmund has asserted his right under
the Copyright, Designs and Patents Act, 1988
to be identified as the author of this work

First published in the United Kingdom in 1993 by
Kensington West Productions

A CIP catalogue record for this book is available
from the British Library
ISBN 1 871349 51 6

Designed by Rob Kelland at Allsport
Typeset in Perpetua and Twentieth Century
Colour reproduction by Trinity Graphic, Hong Kong
Printed and bound in Scotland by Bath Press Colourbooks

PING ® is a registered Trade Mark of
Karsten Manufacturing Corporation

PHOTOGRAPHIC CREDITS

Allsport: 11, 42, 43 (top), 45, 47, 95, 96, 97 (right), 102, 125, 130, 140;
Simon Bruty/Allsport: 122-123, 134; **Dave Cannon/Allsport:** front cover (main), 24, 28, 29, 31, 32,
90-91; **Chris Cole/Allsport:** 103, 104, 107, 109, 137; **Michael Hobbs/Allsport:** 38;
Ken Levine/Allsport USA: 127; **Steve Munday/Allsport:** 20-21, 22, 26, 30, 39, 57, 97 (left), 144;
Gary Newkirk/Allsport USA: 15 (main); **Gary M. Prior:** 101 (inset); **Steve Rose/Allsport:** 17;
Richard Saker/Allsport: 115 (main); **Rick Stewart/Allsport USA:** front cover (lower centre),
back cover (top), 8-9, 13, 16 (main), 56 (top), 66, 67 (main), 80, 89, 138; **Anton Want/Allsport:** 79, 83,
105, 106, 124; **Rick Bullock:** 131; **Michael C. Cohen:** 62 (right), 67 (right), 84; **Du Maurier Ltd
Library:** 70; **Bob Ewell:** 10, 18, 19, 48-49, 50, 53, 54, 55, 58-59, 61, 62 (main), 65 (both), 68, 69, 75,
77, 78, 135, 145; **Matthew Harris:** 16 (left), 51, 86; **Rob Griffin:** 12 (right), 52 (left), 63, 64, 72, 87,
136; **Steve Murphy:** 52 (right); **Scott Lindsay:** 73; **Debbie Newcombe:** 14, 36-37, 98;
Mark Newcombe: front cover (lower left, lower right), back cover (bottom), 4, 12 (left), 15 (right), 23, 25,
35, 40, 41, 43 (bottom), 44 (both), 56 (left), 93, 94, 99, 100-101, 110, 112-113, 115 (left), 117, 118, 119,
121, 129, 132, 139, 141, 142, 143

Contents

All text by Nick Edmund unless otherwise credited

A Welcome

From Karsten and Louise Solheim

Women's golf took global strides in 1992 and we are very happy to play a role in preserving some of the wonderful memories in this, the first edition of the *PING Women's Golf Year.*

Editor Nick Edmund, along with a noteworthy list of contributing writers, have brilliantly detailed the events and personalities that shaped women's golf in 1992. From the amateur ranks to the professionals, the players provided one memorable moment after another - most of which are captured in glorious form by some of the world's premier photographers on the following pages.

We are grateful to have Mickey Walker as author of the foreword. A long-time friend of our company, Mickey is one of the pioneers of women's professional golf in Europe. In her role as Solheim Cup captain, she motivated a team to a victory that may be, as she said herself, one of the greatest sporting achievements of the century. Whatever the outcome's place in the history books, it will forever be etched in our memories. We now eagerly await the '94 Solheim Cup match at The Greenbrier in White Sulphur Springs, West Virginia.

A book of this type and quality is long overdue. Women's golf must not be overlooked; the calibre of play and its marvellous personalities provide so many interesting stories. For these reasons, we supported and encouraged Nick's project from its inception. We're committed to help bring women's golf, both amateur and professional, to the highest level, and we think this book is a step in the right direction.

Enjoy the book and the 1993 season. if it's anything like last year, you'll know why we're true believers in women's golf.

KARSTEN AND LOUISE SOLHEIM

Foreword

Most top class golf these days is played by individuals for personal glory and gain, and whilst the general public often feel reflected glory by association, for instance the British feel proud of Laura Davies and Americans idolise Nancy Lopez, there is nothing that comes close to the emotion generated by international team golf.

As Captain of the winning 1992 European Solheim Cup team at Dalmahoy, I was privileged to be part of the occasion and to share the overwhelming joy experienced by our players and the many wonderful supporters. At the time I said that the victory was one of the major sporting achievements of the century, and now, some months after the event, I still believe that it is.

1992 was truly a watershed year for women's team golf. At Hoylake the Great Britain and Ireland Curtis Cup side scored a narrow victory in a magnificently fought contest; Caroline Hall's winning 4 iron to the 18th green was an outstanding shot, and one that capped a marvellous all-round team performance.

In America, Dottie Mochrie won several tournaments, including her first Major championship, and was the leading money winner on the LPGA Tour. Patty Sheehan, meanwhile, was crowning a glorious career with a popular win in the US Open following a playoff with Juli Inkster. Patty went on to win the Weetabix Women's British Open, becoming the first woman to capture both the US and British Open titles in the same season.

On the WPG European Tour Laura Davies excelled, winning three events and topping the money list for the third time. She has a phenomenal natural talent for the game and was an inspiration to the rest of the home side in the Solheim Cup. Swedish players, notably Helen Alfredsson, shone in all corners of the globe last year. Helen won in Germany, Sweden and Japan, was named Rookie of the Year in America and then combined with Liselotte Neumann to win the end of season Sunrise World Cup in Taiwan; and who will ever forget the moment when Catrin Nilsmark holed the winning putt at Dalmahoy!

This first Women's Golf Year book records in colourful detail all of these exciting happenings - plus much more - and I am delighted that Ping are sponsoring it as there are no greater supporters of women's golf than Karsten Solheim and his family.

I look forward to 1993 with great hopes for women's golf, and naturally will be especially interested in the worldwide progress of the European players with a view to selecting the 1994 Solheim Cup team.

Happy golfing!

MICKEY WALKER

Ping Women's Golf Year

5

'Golfing Desiderata'

GO PLACIDLY amid the heather and the gorse and remember what peace there may be on the fairway. As far as possible without surrender be on good terms with all golfers. Remember to replace your divots and to repair your pitch marks; and listen to elder members, even the dull and ignorant; they all have their story. Avoid loud and aggressive caddies they are vexatious to the spirit.

If you compare your score with others you may become vain and bitter, for there will always be greater and lesser golfers than yourself. Enjoy your pars as well as your birdies. Keep interested in your handicap, however humble; it is a real possession in the changing fortunes of time. Exercise caution with your teeshots for the fairways may be riddled with hidden pot-bunkers. But let this not discourage you from swinging freely; many shots have found the green from thick rough and always there is the hope of a long putt.

Stay calm. Especially avoid losing your temper. Never be cynical about plus fours; for in the face of all aridity and disenchantment, they are as perennial as the tweaked three-footer. Take kindly the counsel of the years, gracefully surrendering the long drives of youth. Nurture strength from your short game to shield you in sudden misfortune. But do not distress yourself with imaginings. Many shots are wasted through fear of slicing and hooking.

With your Brassie and your Mashie and your new Ping putter be content with yourself. You are a part of the links no less than the sandhills and the rabbit scrapes; you have a right to golf here. And whether or not it is clear to you, no doubt the golf links is unfolding as it should. Therefore be at peace with your game, whatever you conceive it to be and whatever the weather, come rain or shine, be at peace with your soul. With all its sham, drudgery and broken dreams, it is still a beautiful game. Be cheerful, strive to be happy.

Discovered on a Gravestone, near St Andrews, Scotland c. 1750

N.E.E.

Introduction

By Nick Edmund

The idea for this book was conceived in a bookshop. Actually in a sports bookshop, while glancing at the various golfing guides and annuals. Of the many titles, how many do you think were dedicated to women's golf? Exactly, not one. These days, it seems, to launch an attractively produced, competitively priced golf annual one needs an able publisher and a generous sponsor. To get a book of this nature off the ground - the very first of its type, we believe - ability and generosity had to be mixed in with imagination and courage. As editor, I would therefore immediately like to thank our publisher, Kensington West Productions, and especially our sponsor, Karsten Manufacturing Corporation, the Phoenix-based creators of Ping golf equipment, for demonstrating their imagination and courage in supporting the project, and so making this book happen.

From the sporting and skilful manner in which it is played to the colour and thrill of the action, women's golf has much to shout about and much to show off. Our book is simply an attempt to help with the shouting and the showing off.

The first *PING Women's Golf Year* surveys the world of women's golf as season 1992 passes into season 1993. The book has seven chapters, in which are detailed the exploits of the best female practitioners of the game - amateur and professional - as they embark on the year's major tournaments and matches. The golf seasons in Europe and America are explored in detail and there are special sections highlighting the Solheim and Curtis Cups. Golf in 'the rest of the world' is not forgotten either and the closing chapter looks forward to the big events of 1993.

Having thanked our sponsor and publisher, I would next like to thank Mickey Walker for providing the book's foreword and our international collection of contributing journalists and photographers. I hope you will agree that the book is beautifully illustrated and I would particularly like to single out the photographic contributions of Dave Cannon and his Allsport colleagues, as well as Mark Newcombe and Bob Ewell. The finished product would not be half as attractive either without the considerable input of designer, Rob Kelland, and nor could it have been produced in the time it was without the support of the leading sports picture agency, Allsport, who kindly allowed the book to be put together on their premises; from super-fast typist Julie Kay to UK Managing Director, Adrian Murrell, I am extremely grateful to them.

NICK EDMUND

1992
A Memorable Season

1992
A Memorable Season

Season? It rained persistently in the Solheim Cup, it rained mightily in the Curtis Cup and it rained even more mightily in the World Cup. It soaked at the start of the British Open and it soaked whenever it pleased at the US Open. Yet for all the untimely and unwelcome precipitation, the golfing gods smiled - and the sun really did shine - on the world of

'I felt like I had to do something', said Betsy King

women's golf in 1992. Of course the gods were selective with their smiles, but by and large, women's golf prospered and advanced happily forwards in season '92.

It was a year that frequently afforded an illustration of that ancient proverb, 'an old head on young shoulders' and, an ungenerous person might suggest, the odd hint of the opposite.

During the final moments of the Solheim Cup, the young and inexperienced Swede, Catrin Nilsmark, played heroically to beat her American opponent Meg Mallon and so clinch the winning point for the home side. Nilsmark could at least gain strength from the knowledge that behind her, two of her European team-mates were also heading towards likely victories. At Hoylake in the Curtis Cup, the only support that her team-mates could give to 18-year-old Caroline Hall as she played the decisive final hole in the final match was to wish her 'the Best of British Luck'. But like Nilsmark, Hall produced the necessary strokes and so both earned for themselves and their teams a significant place in history.

American Betsy King is roughly twice Caroline Hall's age and she has long been assured of more than a fleeting mention in the annals of women's golf. King is acknowledged as one of the greats of the modern game and is widely regarded as being one of the toughest competitors around, a woman possessed of an inner steel. Cool King thrives on pressure, but when the pressure is off, say, when she's about to win a fifth Major championship by 11 strokes, she goes on a wild walkabout - high-fiving, low-fiving, slapping hands with all and sundry.

If King's emotional display at the 72nd

Year' for their respective continents.

The exploits of Mochrie and Davies are comprehensively detailed in this book and interesting insights into 'what makes them tick' are provided by Sonja Steptoe and Patricia Davies. Read on, then, and you will discover why Laura's adopted middle name

hole of the Mazda LPGA Championship was one of the most memorable (and surprising) moments of 1992, her performance over the preceeding 71 holes at Bethesda was more momentous. It was, in the opinion of many, the individual performance of the season. That week she was, quite simply, in a class of her own. Her caddie summed it up nicely at the time when he remarked, 'the way Betsy is playing, Rin Tin Tin could carry her clubs and it wouldn't make any difference.'

Catrin and Caroline were the heroines of the moment and King was majestic for a week but we have chosen Dottie Mochrie and Laura Davies as our 'Golfers of the

is 'inspiration' and why no one is ever likely to forget that Dottie's maiden name was Pepper.

Walking into history — Caroline Hall at the 27th Curtis Cup

With Mochrie and Davies claiming both their home tour's money list and stroke average titles (never mind the American's first Major triumph in the Dinah Shore and the English woman's amazing performance at Dalmahoy), the 'Golfer of the Year' selections might appear to have been a formality; in fact each was a very close thing. Two other candidates had strong claims, namely America's Patty Sheehan and Sweden's Helen Alfredsson. Neither dominated a tour in the way that Mochrie and Davies did, but in terms of world-wide achievement Patty and Helen were arguably the major players of 1992. Sheehan had a roller coaster type year - brilliant one moment, ordinary the next. She alone won individual titles in three continents - and

For Helen Alfredsson, 1992 was nothing less than an *annus mirabilis* (or whatever the Swedish equivalent might be). At the beginning of the year she was widely regarded as a very promising player: Rookie of the Year in Europe in 1989; winner of the British Open in 1990 - her first

Laura Davies — our 'European Golfer of the Year' – during her finest week

what titles! They included a unique US-British Open double. She won on the Japanese tour in the spring, then went quiet for a while; she took the LPGA Tour by storm in the summer, winning three times in five weeks, including the US Open at Oakmont and a nine stroke victory in the Rochester International (she produced middle rounds of 65-63), then went quiet again; in late September she crossed the Atlantic and captured the Weetabix British Open, only to lose her form again a week later at Dalmahoy where she won just one half point in the Solheim Cup.

tournament success - and second place in the European Order of Merit in 1991. By the end of 1992 Helen Alfredsson was one of the best players in the world.

Helen had won herself an LPGA Tour card in late 1991 and was determined to establish herself as a force to be reckoned with in both Europe and America. She certainly didn't waste time! She came sixth on her LPGA debut, after leading the tournament for much of the first three days; in two later events she was leading going into the final two holes but again narrowly missed out; she performed well in the

Dottie Mochrie — our 'American Golfer of the Year' – during her finest week

Majors and claimed the LPGA Rookie of the Year Award, finishing 16th on the Money List. What was more remarkable though, was that she achieved all this while at the same time pursuing Laura Davies for most of the honours and prizes in Europe. She won twice on that continent - once in front of her home fans in Sweden and once in Germany at the Hennessy Cup. In the latter she produced magnificent third and fourth rounds of 67-66 (she was 12 under par for her last 27 holes), winning the tournament with dramatic birdies at the 71st and 72nd holes. Like Davies, Alfredsson was undefeated in October's Solheim Cup, but her season was still far from over as she then travelled to Taiwan and teamed up with Lotte Neumann to win the World Team Cup for Sweden, before heading on to

Japan, where she demolished a strong field to win a prestigious Japanese LPGA Tour event by five shots with rounds of 64-68-68. How do you follow a season like that?

There was very nearly a fifth player to consider too - America's Juli Inkster. *But for* Sheehan and Mochrie holing birdie putts on the final green of the Dinah Shore and the US Open championships, she would have collected two Major titles last year. To Inkster then must go the dubious accolade, 'Golfing Bridesmaid of 1992'.

If the likes of Sheehan and King have been forced to make room for the likes of Mochrie and Alfredsson, so in the not too distant future, might the latter have to share some of their recently won ground with a

The mighty oak of Oakmont... Patty Sheehan in action at the Women's US Open

collection of exceptionally gifted young players - an international array of potential stars who appear to be as determined as they are dynamic.

In Europe, 1992 saw the emergence of 19-year-old Sandrine Mendiburu from France and first tournament wins for fellow

notwithstanding the Great Britain and Ireland Curtis Cup victory, it is fair to say that these two brilliant young players dominated women's amateur golf in 1992. Both Sorenstam and Goetze are set to take the professional plunge in 1993, which in the Georgian golfer's case will mean

(Opposite page)
Mademoiselle
Mendiburu — one of the
great hopes of French
(and European) golf;
(above) America's
Vicki Goetze and (left)
Brandie Burton

French player Valerie Michaud and the Italian Stefania Croce (both of whom are only slightly older than Mendiburu). Meanwhile, Sweden's Annika Sorenstam has been sharing top billing on the US college golf scene with the double-US Amateur champion, Vicki Goetze. Indeed,

renewing a rivalry with Brandie Burton whom she beat in the final of the 1989 US Amateur Championship. Burton is a leading member of the 'twentysomethings' club, which in the first half of 1992 threatened to turn the LPGA Tour on its head.

These are exciting times to be following

the progress of women's golf, for not only is it fascinating to view the struggle between the emerging and the established, but also because so many of the characters in this unfolding drama are blessed with interesting or colourful personalities. The leading women do not often like to be compared with their male counterparts - their golf speaks for itself - but in the matter of personalities it is worth asking where are the Mochries, Alfredssons, Descampes and McGanns of the men's game?

And who is there to compare with Nancy Lopez? In 1992 Lopez won twice on the

Golf needs its personalities — meet 'fiery' Florence Descampe (above) and 'mad-hatter' Michelle McGann (right)

LPGA Tour, lifting her tally of US victories close to the half century mark. In August she was honoured with the award, '1992 Ambassador of Golf'. Such is her standing in the game that perhaps the biggest disappointment of the year was that Lopez was not at Dalmahoy in October to grace

European golf could not possibly have received a greater boost.

Some Americans may not care to be reminded of the occasion too often, but Mickey's comment is, in its way, an enormous compliment to the quality and reputation of the American team. In the

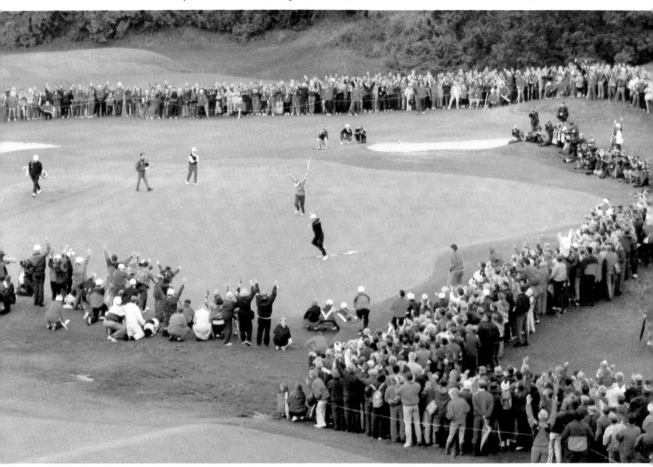

the Solheim Cup. Whether she would have effected the outcome is, however, another matter. In her Foreword to this book, Mickey Walker restates her belief that the European success in the 2nd Solheim Cup was, 'one of the major sporting achievements of the century'. Without doubt, the cause, and one hopes course, of

long term women's golf in America will surely benefit from there being a strong game in Europe. And if golf is to deserve its growing reputation as the greatest game in the world then it must surely be great all over the world. Women's golf certainly was in 1992.

Catrin Nilsmark and **'The Moment'**

World Rankings: The Ping Leaderboard

AS OF 31 DECEMBER 1992

POSITION		POINTS TOTAL
1	Dottie Mochrie (USA)	232.20
2	Patty Sheehan (USA)	175.50
3	Betsy King (USA)	142.75
4	Laura Davies (GB)	141.60
5	Juli Inkster (USA)	134.90
6	Ayako Okamoto (Japan)	128.50
7	Helen Alfredsson (Sweden)	124.50
8	Danielle Ammaccapane (USA)	123.90
9	Brandie Burton (USA)	123.80
10	Colleen Walker (USA)	116.00
11	Meg Mallon (USA)	113.50
12	Nancy Lopez (USA)	110.70
13	Beth Daniel (USA)	95.90
14	Judy Dickinson (USA)	94.50
15	Patti Rizzo (USA)	87.75
16	Sherri Steinhauer (USA)	87.60
17	Florence Descampe (Belgium)	80.00
18	Liselotte Neumann (Sweden)	77.50
19	Donna Andrews (USA)	76.65
20	Dawn Coe-Jones (Canada)	76.50
21	Junko Yasui (Japan)	69.80
22	Ai-Yu Tu (Taiwan)	69.50
23	Deb Richard (USA)	67.90
24	Young-Me Lee (Taiwan)	67.50
25	Ikuyo Shiotani (Japan)	66.00
26	Dana Lofland (USA)	65.40
27	Bie-Shyun Huang (Taiwan)	58.50
28	Alison Nicholas (GB)	58.35
29	Michelle McGann (USA)	57.35
30	Nayoko Yoshikawa (Japan)	53.80
31	Corinne Dibnah (Australia)	52.25
32	Trish Johnson (GB)	50.00
33	Karen Lunn (Australia)	48.50
34	Pat Bradley (USA)	48.10
35	Jane Geddes (USA)	48.00
36	Rosie Jones (USA)	47.30
37	Michiko Hattori (Japan)	47.00
38	Jennifer Sevil (Australia)	45.00
39	Barb Mucha (USA)	44.10
40	Missie Berteotti (USA)	44.05
41	Nancy Scranton (USA)	43.80
42	Kristi Albers (USA)	42.30
43	Ok-Hee Ku (Korea)	42.15
44	Aki Nakano (Japan)	42.00
45	Tammie Green (USA)	41.75
46	Jane Crafter (Australia)	39.00
47	Shelley Hamlin (USA)	39.00
48	Yuko Moriguchi (Japan)	37.80
49	JoAnne Carner (USA)	37.30
50	Alice Ritzman (USA)	36.90

Seventh heaven — Sweden's rising star, Helen Alfredsson (opposite) and the world's number one Dottie Mochrie

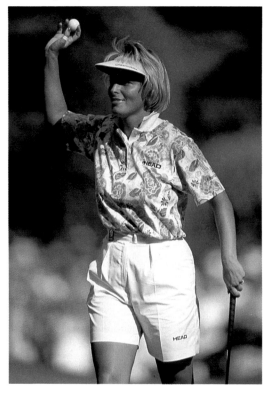

*The Ping Leaderboard is a world-wide ranking table designed to reflect players' performances over a rolling 12 month period

2

The Solheim Cup

The Solheim Cup

An Introduction

Of all the great team events in the world of golf the Solheim Cup is the baby of the family. It is easy to suppose that a biennial match between the best women professionals in America and their counterparts from Europe was an inevitability, but for one thing it needed people of vision and determination to make it happen and, initially of course, it needed a catalyst. The latter was provided when Laura Davies and Liselotte Neumann won the US Women's Open in successive years in the late 1980s; prior to their victories it was felt that there could be no contest simply

because it would be precisely that - no contest. The American players, whose games, never mind natural competitiveness, were constantly being primed on a thriving LPGA Tour, appeared to inhabit a different golfing planet from the Europeans and their fledgling circuit.

Regarding the first mentioned prerequisite, perhaps to vision and determination one should add the word support, for without the generous encouragement of Karsten Solheim, his family and their company, the dream might never have materialised.

The European team that travelled to Lake

The US won the 1st Solheim Cup match by 11 ½ - 4 ½; Nancy Lopez and Cathy Gerring (neither of whom played at Dalmahoy) celebrate their success at Lake Nona, Florida

Nona in November 1990 was comprehensively beaten, but the players certainly contested every point. In fact, they won 4½ - which is 4½ more than one or two cynical commentators had predicted. 'Each point was like a monumental achievement', said European captain Mickey Walker at the time. More significantly, the visitors understood how it was that they lost the 11½ points: to some extent, it was because they were genuinely in awe of several of the Americans (Nancy Lopez-worshipping was particularly rife), and it was partly because in their play on and around the greens the Americans really were far superior.

The two lessons for the Europeans to take home from Lake Nona then, were (i) they must urgently discover some self-belief, and (ii) they must practise, practise and practise the short game.

The two years flew by, and when the two sets of teams prepared to head for Scotland last September for the 2nd Solheim Cup match the mood among the European players, and especially their captain, was altogether different. 'I have got a fantastic team. I believe we can go to Dalmahoy and win,' declared Mickey Walker - who had obviously watched them practise, practise and practise...

Scotland's Dale Reid drives against the splendid backdrop of Dalmahoy's 18th century mansion

The 2nd Solheim Cup

2 - 4 OCTOBER 1992 • DALMAHOY HOTEL G & CC, LOTHIAN, SCOTLAND
FORMAT: DAY ONE, FOURSOMES; DAY TWO, FOURBALLS; DAY THREE, SINGLES
CAPTAINS: EUROPE, MICKEY WALKER; USA, ALICE MILLER (STANDING IN FOR KATHY WHITWORTH)

It was entirely appropriate that the famous Red Arrows display team should have soared overhead and graced the opening ceremony at the second Solheim Cup. The Red Arrows, those incredible acrobats of the air, possess, and perhaps symbolise, many of life's finer qualities: individual courage, team spirit, dogged determination and panache. Though their multi-coloured

Inseparable and unbeatable: Laura Davies and Alison Nicholas

sky trails didn't linger in the Scottish air for long, it was as if such qualities somehow filtered down and affected the assembled cast of 20. Throughout three historic days at Dalmahoy all of these qualities were displayed in great abundance.

Hyperbole? I offer no apologies. This Solheim Cup was all about superlatives. Several days before the match began some mighty adjectives were being used to describe the strength (or at least the on-paper strength) of the visiting American team. With 143 LPGA Tour titles liberally sprinkled among them, and no fewer than 20 Major championships - never mind some 25 million dollars in prize money - it was indeed a formidable line-up.

Extreme adjectives were also being bandied about to highlight the degree of conviction and sheer determination of the European players. It was even suggested that Mickey Walker and her players had thought about nothing else for the past two years. Wanting to win badly was one thing of course, but if the Europeans were to have a real prospect of overturning Alice Miller's all-stars they knew that they would have to play the best golf of their lives.

With hindsight, it was also wholly appropriate that the contest should have commenced with a winning birdie from the Laura Davies and Alison Nicholas partnership. None of the other foursome pairings could do likewise and the Anglo-

Europeans promptly birdied their second hole to go two up.

When it comes to trying to read the minds of the two Captains, the one thing we can be fairly confident about is that Mickey Walker didn't give too much thought as to whether or not to partner Davies with Nicholas: Gilbert and Sullivan, Morecambe and Wise, Davies and Nicholas... The choices she did make - and kept faith with for the first two days - were to pair the two Swedes, Helen Alfredsson and Lotte Neumann, the two Scots, Dale Reid and Pam Wright and to link the flamboyant Belgian, Florence Descampe with the reliable Trish Johnson, arguably Britain's number two player behind Davies. Alice Miller, however, was prepared to 'pick and mix' a little bit to ensure that all 10 of her players participated in the first two days. Again, with the benefit of hindsight, such generosity may have been the Americans' undoing.

The opening birdies of Davies and Nicholas gave them an early lead over Betsy King and Beth Daniel, the kind of pairing that would have had the Europeans quaking in their spikes at Lake Nona in 1990. How do you play against Betsy and Beth? The Davies and Nicholas approach at Dalmahoy was to launch a cavalier assault. This is how they scored over their first 10 holes (remembering that this was a foursome not a fourball), birdie - birdie - bogey - par - bogey - par - birdie - birdie - birdie - birdie. Women's golf always was boring! Most golfers would crumble under such an onslaught but not King and Daniel and in the end the European pair had to halve the last to win a tremendous match 1 up. A close shave, but the prized scalp was theirs.

The magnificent run of early birdies (six in the first 10 holes) seemed to inspire the

Support from the sidelines was never in short supply at Dalmahoy

P i n g   W o m e n ' s   G o l f   Y e a r

When it rained (and it did frequently) multi-coloured mushrooms encircled every green in the first 10 holes) seemed to inspire the Europeans playing directly behind and at about the same time that Davies and Nicholas were shaking hands with King and Daniel, Alfredsson and Neumann were doing likewise having defeated the second awesome duo of Dottie (world's number one) Mochrie and Pat (Hall of Fame) Bradley by 2 and 1.

The third and fourth matches, however, appeared to be going America's way. Danielle Ammaccapane and Meg Mallon were never behind against Descampe and Johnson - they eventually hung on to win 1 up, and Patty Sheehan and Juli Inkster advanced to 3 up after 10 holes against the best named pair of all, Reid and Wright. Spurred on by a partisan Scottish gallery, the home pair battled back against the two players who earlier in the summer finished first and second in the US Open, and eventually snatched a dramatic half enabling Europe to lead 2½ - 1½ at the end of the first day.

It had rained for much of Friday and it proceeded to rain for much of Saturday - which suited Laura Davies to a tee. The wetter the course, the longer the course and given that Laura could clout the ball about 30 yards further than any one else at Dalmahoy it gave her a tremendous advantage, particularly on some of the par fives which in the water-logged conditions she alone could reach in two.

One could say that the tactics employed by Davies and Nicholas in the opening second day fourball were fairly crude in that Nicholas would 'hit one safely down the middle' leaving Davies 'free to have an

Making quite an impact:
Danielle Ammaccapane
— a polished swing and
a patriotic pullover

P i n g   W o m e n ' s   G o l f   Y e a r

almighty smash'. Crude or not, it worked superbly because Davies was not only crashing her drives into oblivion but hitting them unerringly straight into the bargain, moreover, somebody had apparently borrowed her putter overnight and sprinkled it with magic dust. She was as lethal on the greens as she was off the tee.

So the English pair once again led from the front and with a better ball round of 66 won a second vital point for Europe, this time at the expense of Sheehan and Inkster. (Sheehan must have wondered how this could possibly be the same Laura Davies she had beaten by 18 strokes at Woburn just six days previously!).

Winning Solheim Cup debuts for Brandie Burton and Deb Richard seemed likely in the second Saturday fourball match when they won the 13th and 14th holes to go 2 up against Johnson and Descampe, but the Europeans immediately struck back with birdies at the 15th and 16th holes and the match was halved.

Some superb golf on the front nine enabled Mallon and King to establish a four hole lead over Reid and Wright before the battling Scots launched a late charge for the second day running. This time, however, they had left themselves too much to do and were eventually beaten on the final green. With the match score standing at 4-3, the result of the final fourball between Alfredsson and Neumann and Bradley and Mochrie was clearly extremely important to both sides. It turned out to be a wonderful game which swung first one way then the other and finally ended all-square when Pat Bradley struck her approach stone dead at the 18th for a birdie three and Neumann agonisingly missed from inside five feet for the win. It is accepted that even Swedes can

be emotional in such circumstances.

Perfectly poised at 4½ - 3½ in favour of Europe, both teams had reason to feel confident of victory that evening; there were, after all, still 10 points to play for in the Sunday singles. The commentators who had waxed lyrical over the statistical might

of the American team were in their element when they analysed some of the pairings for Sunday. Trish Johnson v the US and British Open champion, Patty Sheehan, for instance; and what about Pam Wright v Pat Bradley, the

Lotte Neumann's miss has just made the score 4½ to 3½ at the end of the second day

winner of six Majors and over four million dollars? Or Catrin Nilsmark, who hadn't yet played a match in the Solheim Cup (or won a European Tour event for that matter) v Meg Mallon, the US Open and LPGA champion of 1991 and Dale Reid v Dottie Mochrie? Surely these were four points that

best move would be to lead off once again with Laura Davies and to send Helen Alfredsson out immediately behind her; if they could maintain their form of the first two days and win, then Europe would only need three more points from the existing eight singles for a famous victory.

Coming to terms with defeat: stunned and overcome members of the US team

had stars and stripes drawn all over them? Incredibly, not one of them did. In her wildest dreams Mickey Walker cannot have imagined that her players could win all of those matches and go on to take seven of the 10 singles points. She afterwards admitted to being in a state of shock, and that was probably the understatement of the week.

Walker had judged correctly that her

Davies and Alfredsson didn't let her down - nor did the eight who followed. Davies produced a sensational beginning when she powered two woods into the heart of the green at the par five 1st, a feat nobody else came close to achieving, and in fact only Catrin Nilsmark matched her opening birdie. To her credit, Burton clung to Davies' coat-tails, and with a superb eagle at the 9th, drew level at the turn, but then Laura suddenly unleashed four birdies on the back nine to gain a convincing 4 and 2 victory. Her dynamic performance appeared to create a domino effect. And it was the Americans who were knocked over.

Danielle Ammaccapane halved the first seven holes of her match with Alfredsson but then lost four in a row as the Swede charged to a 4 and 3 success. Alfredsson

Nilsmark who outplayed the hitherto unbeaten Meg Mallon, and was three under par as she stood 3 up on the 16th fairway, aware that a victory in her match would win the Solheim Cup for Europe. With all that pressure on her young shoulders she struck an arrow-straight three iron to within 20

hadn't dropped a single stroke all day and was three under par when the match finished (Davies had been five under). But they, by no means, had a monopoly of the low scoring: after a shaky six at the 1st, Trish Johnson played the remainder of her match against Patty Sheehan in four under par; Pam Wright produced four birdies in five holes to storm past Pat Bradley and Lotte Neumann was three under in defeating Betsy King. The biggest surprise though was surely the amazing performance of Catrin

feet of the flag. In that shot was crystallised the performance of the entire team.

The Europeans had played the golf of their lives when it mattered most. There had been both individual courage and team spirit; there had been dogged determination and there had been more than a hint of panache.

Above all, like the Red Arrows in their world, they had proved themselves to be the ultimate team.

Coming to terms with victory: stunned and overjoyed members of the European team

Europe's Captain Mickey Walker savours the proudest moment of her life

2ND SOLHEIM CUP

2 - 4 OCTOBER 1992 • DALMAHOY HOTEL G & CC, LOTHIAN, SCOTLAND

EUROPE	MATCHES	USA	MATCHES
FOURSOMES (FRIDAY)			
L. Davies & A. Nicholas (1 up)	1	B. King & B. Daniel	0
L. Neumann & H. Alfredsson (2 & 1)	1	P. Bradley & D. Mochrie	0
F. Descampe & T. Johnson	0	D. Ammaccapane & M. Mallon (1 up)	1
D. Reid & P. Wright	½	P. Sheehan & J. Inkster	½
FOURBALLS (SATURDAY)			
L. Davies & A. Nicholas (1 up)	1	P. Sheehan & J. Inkster	0
F. Descampe & T. Johnson	½	B. Burton & D. Richard	½
P. Wright & D. Reid	0	M. Mallon & B. King (1 up)	1
L. Neumann & H. Alfredsson	½	P. Bradley & D. Mochrie	½
SINGLES (SUNDAY)			
L. Davies (4 & 2)	1	B. Burton	0
H. Alfredsson (4 & 3)	1	D. Ammaccapane	0
T. Johnson (2 & 1)	1	P. Sheehan	0
A. Nicholas	0	J. Inkster (3 & 2)	1
F. Descampe	0	B. Daniel (2 & 1)	1
P. Wright (4 & 3)	1	P. Bradley	0
C. Nilsmark (3 & 2)	1	M. Mallon	0
K. Douglas	0	D. Richard (7 & 6)	1
L. Neumann (2 & 1)	1	B. King	0
D. Reid (3 & 2)	1	D. Mochrie	0
EUROPE 11½		**USA 6½**	

P i n g   W o m e n ' s   G o l f   Y e a r

The Wider Picture and a Greater Goal

A Reflection by Lauren St John

Long before Catrin Nilsmark of Sweden holed the putt that won the Solheim Cup for Europe, teams of women golfers were bringing glory to their nations.

It all began soon after the turn of the century with the Battle of the Tempestuous Petticoats, as it was irreverently known, an informal team match between seven American amateur women golfers and seven British. At that time, however, the latter weren't considered the underdogs - as they have been for much of the time since - they came and they saw on equal terms with the Americans, and the team that conquered was simply the best on the day.

In 1905 it was the British players who proved dominant. Captained by Lottie Dod, winner of the Ladies' Open Championship, not to mention five Wimbledon tennis titles, they swept to a 6-1 victory at Cromer Golf Club in Norfolk, England. Curiously enough, given that they had made the arduous crossing in vain, the matches had most impact on two members of the vanquished American team, namely Harriot and Margaret Curtis.

Thrilled by the standard of play the competition inspired, and by the pervading spirit of goodwill the Curtis sisters became determined to create a regular match between the two nations. In 1927 they purchased a trophy, but it was not until five years later that their dream came true and the Curtis Cup was born.

The early days of women's team golf, amateur as well as professional, draw inevitable comparison with the equivalent men's team events, the Walker and Ryder Cups. The Ryder Cup, for example, owed its existence to a British seed merchant by the name of Samuel Ryder, who had taken up golf for the good of his health. Such was Ryder's respect for professional golfers and love of the game that in 1926 he donated a trophy to the Professional Golfers' Association for use in an international match, the purpose of which was to foster goodwill between the golfers of the United States and Great Britain and Ireland.

That his wish was fulfilled is illustrated by the events of the 1969 match at Royal Birkdale. Jack Nicklaus and Tony Jacklin had arrived at the final green all-square, the outcome of the Ryder Cup riding on their shoulders. The Golden Bear had hit his first putt about four feet past the hole, while Jacklin was a couple of feet short. Nicklaus sank his putt, walked over to the Englishman and said 'I don't think you would have missed that putt, but in these circumstances I would never give you the opportunity.' And thus the Ryder Cup was drawn for the first time in history.

By 1983, at which point the competition was already almost 56 years old, the Europeans (as the Great Britain and Ireland side became in 1979) had only won twice, once in 1929 and once in 1957. The parallels between what happened to turn the tide of fortune for Europe's men professionals in the Ryder Cup and what happened to do the same for the women in the Solheim Cup are extraordinary. In both cases the European players, having previously been intimidated by the might of the Americans, began to cross the Atlantic more frequently and, as they grew in confidence, win on the US Tour. Both teams appointed inspirational leaders - Jacklin captained the Ryder Cup and Mickey Walker the Solheim Cup, and both owed much to the inclusion of an inspirational pairing - Seve Ballesteros and José Maria Olazabal on the one hand, and Laura Davies and Alison Nicholas on the other.

It is strange how, despite the equalising effects of the handicap system, the financial gulf between men's and women's golf is far wider than it is in sports like tennis. What is stranger is that until recent times, the women's game in Europe had not progressed as quickly as it had in the United States. But just as nothing breeds complacency like an abundance of money, so nothing fuels desire like hunger. In amateur golf the Great Britain and Ireland team, tired of an unrelieved diet of failure and commiseration, kicked over the traces and stormed to victory in the Curtis Cup. To date they have won three of the last four matches. In professional golf, players such as Laura Davies were competing and winning on the LPGA Tour in America.

Karsten Solheim, the mastermind behind Ping golf clubs, had been a long-time supporter of women's amateur golf and sponsor of LPGA events when the idea for a professional team event for women was discussed, and his patronage was welcomed.

He wanted to create an event that gathered the best women professionals in Europe and the United States together, engendered good will among golfing nations, and fostered friendship between officials. It was decided that the playing format should be similar to that of the Ryder Cup. There would be foursome matches on the first day, four-ball matches on the second and singles on the third. The teams would play for a magnificent crystal trophy, mouth-blown and hand-cut by a team of designers at the Waterford Crystal Company in Ireland.

In 1990 two teams of the finest women golfers in the world gathered at Lake Nona Golf Club in Orlando, Florida for the inaugural Solheim Cup. Seven of the participants had earlier played in Curtis Cup matches. 'A whirlwind experience,' was how European Captain, Mickey Walker later described that first contest even though Europe had been defeated 11½ - 4½, for she felt it had been one of the best experiences of her life. 'I never felt that we had been thrashed,' she said. 'At the end, I was more elated than depressed.'

When the teams met for the second time at Dalmahoy Hotel Golf & Country Club, near Edinburgh, it was clear from the outset that there had been a sea-change in European morale. 'There is nothing, absolutely nothing, to beat the Solheim Cup,' enthused Helen Alfredsson of Sweden. 'I was desperate to play in it for a second time.' In the interim period between the first and second matches a host of new talent had burgeoned: Florence Descampe, the gifted Belgian, had emerged as a potential superstar, and Alfredsson had been named Rookie of the Year on the LPGA Tour. Davies, meanwhile, was continuing to win tournaments on both sides of the

Atlantic. 'They still respect us,' commented leading American Patty Sheehan, 'but they also respect themselves.'

The Europeans wasted no time in proving her right. They were leading by a point on 2½ to 1½ following the first day's foursomes, and were still ahead after the fourballs were drawn. And on the final day, when more than just pride was at stake, they went out in force and one by one overcame the Americans. Davies defeated Brandie Burton four and two, Alfredsson beat Danielle Ammaccapane, Trish Johnson beat Sheehan, Pam Wright beat Pat Bradley, Liselotte Neumann beat Betsy King, Dale Reid beat Dottie Mochrie and Catrin Nilsmark holed the winning putt for Europe on the 16th green in her match against Meg Mallon.

Afterwards Nilsmark was to say: 'I had no expectations and no fears. I just went out to play each shot as if it were the most important of my life.'

Thus far women's team golf, particularly where the Solheim and Curtis Cups are concerned, has been a credit to almost everyone who has participated in it. 'The Solheim Cup is the epitome of why we play golf,' commented Trish Johnson. The spirit of the matches is reflected in the inscription on the Curtis Cup trophy - 'To stimulate friendly rivalry among the women golfers of many lands' - and in the speech of Margaret Curtis shortly before the Americans set sail for the 1948 Curtis Cup at Royal Birkdale in England. At the farewell dinner she reminded Glenna Collet Vare's team of their responsibility as goodwill ambassadors for their nation as well as for golf. Then she stunned the gathered party by concluding: 'I hope they (GB and Ireland) win this year.'

Peggy Kirk Bell remembered the reaction of her fellow team members at the time: 'Gosh, we thought we were supposed to win!'

Later they realised what Margaret Curtis had meant, just as the Ryder Cup players appreciated what Samuel Ryder had wanted the match he lent his name to to represent, and the Solheim Cup players honoured Karsten Solheim's wish that friendship between nations be uppermost in their minds. These events are not about winning or losing, they are about taking part.

The Curtis Cup

The Curtis Cup

An Introduction

If great sporting occasions merit the greatest venues then the Curtis Cup and Royal Liverpool were made for one another. In a world where so called sportsmen (and women) are prepared to abuse their bodies merely to run faster and throw further, the Curtis Cup, to adopt the words of Mitchell Platts, now Director of Communications for the PGA European Tour, 'remains a shining example of all that is good in sport.'

To be selected to play in the Curtis Cup is one of the greatest honours in the game. Brandie Burton, a finalist in the 1989 US Amateur Championship, and now a rising star on the LPGA Tour, said after playing in the 1990 match at Somerset Hills, New Jersey: 'For myself, I have never known excitement to compare with those two days.' And that 1990 contest wasn't even a close affair!

Imagine then the thrill of playing at Hoylake, home of the Royal Liverpool Golf Club, on a course that has hosted ten Open Championships, including the celebrated Open of 1930 when the incomparable Bobby Jones won the third leg of his incredible Grand Slam. Yes, Hoylake has a history of welcoming great sporting ambassadors and for producing magical moments to savour. The 1992 Curtis Cup significantly enriched that tradition.

Royal Liverpool Golf Club has staged ten British Opens and now one Curtis Cup

· ROLL OF HONOUR ·

YEAR	VENUE	WINNERS	SCORE	YEAR	VENUE	WINNERS	SCORE
1932	Wentworth, England	USA	5½ - 3½	1966	Cascades, USA	USA	13 - 5
1934	Chevy Chase, USA	USA	6½ - 2½	1968	Royal County Down, NI	USA	10½ - 7½
1936	Gleneagles, Scotland	Tied	4½ - 4½	1970	Brae Burn, USA	USA	11½ - 6½
1938	Essex, USA	USA	5½ - 3½	1972	Western Gailes, Scotland	USA	10 - 8
1948	Royal Birkdale, England	USA	6½ - 2½	1974	San Francisco, USA	USA	13 - 5
1950	Buffalo, USA	USA	7½ - 1½	1976	Royal Lytham, England	USA	11½ - 6½
1952	Muirfield, Scotland	GB&I	5 - 4	1978	Apawamis, USA	USA	12 - 6
1954	Merion, USA	USA	6 - 3	1980	St Pierre, Wales	USA	13 - 5
1956	Prince's, England	GB&I	5 - 4	1982	Denver, USA	USA	14½ - 3½
1958	Brae Burn, USA	Tied	4½ - 4½	1984	Muirfield, Scotland	USA	9½ - 8½
1960	Lindrick, England	USA	6½ - 2½	1986	Prairie Dunes, USA	GB&I	13 - 5
1962	Broadmoor, USA	USA	8 - 1	1988	Royal St Georges, England	GB&I	11 - 7
1964	Royal Porthcawl, Wales	USA	10½ - 7½	1990	Somerset Hills, USA	USA	14 - 4
				1992	Royal Liverpool, England	GB&I	10 - 8

P i n g   W o m e n ' s   G o l f   Y e a r

The 27th Curtis Cup

5 - 6 JUNE 1992 • ROYAL LIVERPOOL GC, HOYLAKE, CHESHIRE, ENGLAND
FORMAT: DAY ONE, AM - FOURSOMES; PM - SINGLES; DAY TWO, AM - FOURSOMES; PM - SINGLES
CAPTAINS: GB & IRELAND, LIZ BOATMAN; USA, JUDY OLIVER

*E*veryone expected the wind to blow but even on the north west coast of England it wasn't meant to rain in June - or at least not the way it did on Friday 5th June last year at Hoylake when the proverbial 'cats and dogs' were jettisoned from above. Good old Britain: the first day of the Curtis Cup and it was hot porridge, several layers of clothing and the strongest umbrella you could buy. Yet it was well worth braving the elements, as several thousand hardy spectators will testify, for the golf they saw was rarely less than fascinating.

Amy Fruhwirth helps Vicki Goetze to read between the lines

The 27th Curtis Cup brought together two fairly evenly matched sides. The Americans, captained by Judy Oliver, probably started out marginally as favourites, if only because history was on their side and in 19-year-old Vicki Goetze they had the outstanding amateur player in the world; but on the other hand, Liz Boatman's Great Britain and Ireland team enjoyed strong local support, not to mention home advantage over a very

traditional links type course, one on which its players had practised many times. Thus it was always destined to be a close contest. And how!

Both sides paraded a nice blend of youth and experience. Many of the assembled 16 had participated in the previous biennial encounter at Somerset Hills, New Jersey when the Americans reclaimed the trophy they had so surprisingly lost on home soil four years earlier, by winning in convincing fashion. But sunny Somerset Hills seemed a million miles away as the first drives were hit into the slanting rain at Hoylake in the three first day morning foursomes.

The top match paired the two Halls, Julie and Caroline (both from England but unrelated) against the very strong duo of Vicki Goetze and Amy Fruhwirth (who at least looked related with their similar builds and identical rainwear outfits). Only a few days prior to arriving at stormy Hoylake Goetze had been playing (and winning) an important college championship in Phoenix, Arizona where the temperature had been a steady 90 degrees fahrenheit. With so little time to acclimatise Great Britain and Ireland would have been anticipating, or at least hoping, for a fast start from the Halls in what was inevitably going to be a key opening encounter. It was extremely worrying for home supporters then when the 1st and 2nd holes were won by America, whereupon, wrote Patricia Davies,

'British and Irish hearts must have sunk to the bottom of their Wellingtons.' Home morale was quickly restored, however, for by the time the four players reached the 5th tee the match was all square. It developed into an absorbing contest of which the Halls appeared to have gained control when they stood 2 up with 3 to play.

Behind them the talented Scot, Catriona Lambert, partnering the vastly experienced Vicki Thomas of Wales, had also trailed their opponents on the front nine but after a brilliant eagle at the 14th always looked to have the measure of Leslie Shannon and Sarah Le Brun Ingram - they in fact went on to win 2 and 1 - and in the final game Cheshire's Joanne Morley and Ireland's Claire Hourihane were putting in a superb finish to overhaul Carol Semple Thompson (a veteran of seven Curtis Cup matches) and 20-year-old Tracy Hanson. Incredibly, a 3-0

morning advantage to Great Britain and Ireland suddenly seemed possible, even probable. Despite their lightweight frames, Goetze and Fruhwirth however are made of stern stuff: they cooly weathered the storm and then rallied to capture two of the last three holes so snatching a valuable, if sole, half point for the visitors. Washed out maybe, but at least not whitewashed.

Catriona Lambert extricates herself from the rough

Although the wind remained fierce in the afternoon at least the rain relented for the eagerly awaited six singles matches. The four players who had cheered from the sidelines now stepped onto centre stage, and in fact duelled with one another, with Elaine Farquharson scoring a home victory against Robin Weiss (2 and 1) and Martha Lang aiding the visitors cause by defeating Nicola Buxton (2 holes).

Amy Fruhwirth and Vicki Goetze were again involved in the top two matches and once more they were seesaw affairs. Goetze, 'the mistress of the short game', eventually outputted Julie Hall to record a 3 and 2 victory and ahead of her Fruhwirth established an early lead over Joanne Morley, at which time it looked as if there might be little, if anything, between the two teams come nightfall after all. Midway through the afternoon though, the tide turned dramatically in favour of Liz Boatman's players. Cheered on by a large gallery, Morley, the local favourite, produced a succession of birdies on the back nine and Fruhwirth eventually needed to sink a five foot putt at the 18th for a half. It was infectious: in the final two matches Catriona Lambert birdied the 14th then holed a 35 foot putt on the 16th to close out Semple Thompson 3 and 2, while 18-year-old Caroline Hall produced, 'the best golf I've played in my life' against the unfortunate Leslie Shannon to win by the huge margin of 6 and 5. The English champion was four under par for the 13 holes she played - an extraordinary

achievement in the conditions. It all added up to a 6-3 lead for Great Britain and Ireland at the end of Friday's play. The hot porridge had clearly done the trick even if the champagne was still on ice... and Somerset Hills was now looking about two million miles away.

Home prayers that Friday night would have been for one thing only - three and a half points: anyhow, anyway, anywhere. Three and a half more points for a famous victory; three and a half more points for a place in history. American prayers, on the other hand, would have been for two things: inspiration and sunshine - and they got a fair sprinkling of both when Saturday dawned.

Perhaps the one thing Judy Oliver's side lacked on Saturday was the ability to finish a game off. Each of the three morning foursomes looked to be theirs for the taking; had they done so of course the match would have been all square at lunch with the impetus firmly with the visitors.

In a re-run of Friday morning's epic game, Goetze and Fruhwirth were paired against the Halls in the top match. After 12 holes the Americans, basking beneath a

The bunkers at Hoylake were beautiful to look at – but best avoided!

(Right) American captain, Judy Oliver ponders her next move; (below) Cheshire's Joanne Morley remained undefeated in four games

Phoenix-blue sky, had stormed into a four hole lead with just six holes to play - surely they couldn't let such a lead slip? British birdies and missed putts meant they could and when Fruhwirth failed from no more than a yard at the 18th the Halls had stolen an unlikely half point. In the second match it was always 'nip and tuck' between Hourihane and Morley and Lang and Weiss, but after Lang chipped-in at the 17th it looked as if America might take the spoils, but Hourihane played a superb bunker shot at the last and once again the point was shared. The final foursomes however did produce an American victory when Hanson and Semple Thompson defeated Lambert and Thomas 3 and 2; it gave Semple Thompson a record 12th Curtis Cup point and brought the match score to 7-5.

Needing to win four points from the remaining six singles to retain the trophy, Judy Oliver reckoned her best tactic would be to lead off with the unbeaten Fruhwirth and to play Goetze in the anchor role. To the casual onlooker it must have appeared that the British tactic was to bring on the

Duke of York - Prince Andrew - who made a timely appearance at lunchtime and proceeded to follow the contest most avidly before later presenting the Cup. Boatman's actual plan was to play perhaps her two most consistent players, Morley and Lambert in the first two singles and to gamble on her

Hall made a marvellous birdie at the 16th to draw level with Goetze, having earlier been two down with eight holes to play. The 17th hole was halved and with the match score standing at 9-8 to Great Britain and Ireland Goetze now needed to win the 18th if America was to retain the Cup. The

(Left) Blue skies over a rugged links. (Below) Amazing and amazed — Caroline Hall tries to take it all in

most precocious talent, 18-year-old Caroline Hall, in the final match.

For much of the afternoon it looked as if the visitors might, to use that famous cliché, snatch victory from the jaws of defeat. Only Lambert seemed a certain winner for Great Britain and Ireland (she beat Hanson 6 and 5) but with Thomas, Farquharson and Hourihane all heading towards 2 and 1 defeats by Shannon, Le Brun Ingram and Lang respectively, it was all down to those all-important lead and anchor matches.

Both Fruhwirth and Goetze led their opponents for much of the day but, cheered on by an increasingly excited gallery, Morley and Hall were able to produce their best form over the closing holes. Morley turned her match around superbly to defeat a stunned Fruhwirth on the 17th green and

tension was almost unbearable.

Joanne Morley put an arm around Caroline Hall as she walked to that final tee. At such a moment reality is supposed to run up your spine. But when you are 18 what is reality? Maybe it is the sight of your team mates rushing across the final green to give you a monumental hug.

Liz Boatman receives the Curtis Cup from Prince Andrew

27TH CURTIS CUP

5 - 6 JUNE 1992 • ROYAL LIVERPOOL, HOYLAKE, CHESHIRE, ENGLAND

DAY ONE

FOURSOMES (GB&I first):

J Hall & C Hall halved with A Fruhwirth & V Goetze;

V Thomas & C Lambert bt
   L Shannon & S Le Brun Ingram 2&1;

J Morley & C Hourihane bt T Hanson
   & C Semple Thompson 2&1

SINGLES:

Morley halved with Fruhwirth;

J Hall lost to Goetze 3&2;

E Farquharson bt R Weiss 2&1;

N Buxton lost to M Lang 2 down;

Lambert bt Semple Thompson 3&2;

C Hall bt Shannon 6&5

DAY TWO

FOURSOMES:

J Hall & C Hall halved with Fruhwirth & Goetze;

Hourihane & Morley halved with Lang & Weiss;

Lambert & Thomas lost to Hanson & Semple Thompson 3&2

SINGLES:

Morley bt Fruhwirth 2&1;

Lambert bt Hanson 6&5;

Farquharson lost to Le Brun Ingram 2&1;

Thomas lost to Shannon 2&1;

Hourihane lost to Lang 2&1;

C Hall bt Goetze 1 up

MATCH RESULT: GB&I 10, USA 8

The 'Royal Command' Performance and its aftermath

A Reflection by Lewine Mair

Eighteen year-old Caroline Hall, was playing Vicki Goetze, 19, in the only singles left out on the course in the evening sunshine. They were all square, with everything depending on the outcome of their match and both girls knowing as much.

A few years ago, there would have been American voices as well as British suggesting that a home victory would be good for the match itself, what with America winning all but four of the first 26 contests.

However, Great Britain and Ireland's successive victories in 1986 and 1988 had put an entirely different complexion on the event - and that in spite of the fact that the Americans won the 1990 instalment by a resounding 14-4.

British and American fingernails were thus being chewed in equal measures as Hall and Goetze walked after two fine drives at Hoylake's 18th. The star player of the US side, a wonderfully correct little player in the technical sense, hit her second first.

Accuracy with the fairway woods is arguably Goetze's strongest suit but, on this occasion, she pushed her three-wood into the greenside bunker on the right. Hall, was never in two minds about the four iron she selected for her shot from the edge of the left rough. Thinking to herself, 'It's now or never,' she settled over the ball, kept her head down - and prayed. Her ball covered the flag and dropped on the green to a

rising roar from the 8,000 or so spectators.

Goetze exploded from the sand to 15 feet and missed. Hall made her winning four and the watching Duke of York said, with an expressive shudder, 'I'm glad none of that was up to me!'

Almost inevitably, the Bristol teenager suffered a bit of a reaction in the months that followed but, after a high finish in the British Strokeplay Championship at the end of the year, she followed Elaine Farquharson in turning professional. Joanne Morley was planning on joining them before too long.

That there is a professional tour in Europe is good and bad as far as Britain's Ladies' Golf Union is concerned. Officialdom benefits from having young players seeing the game as a possible career and therefore taking their golf seriously. At the same time, it is hardly wholly satisfying that players should use LGU coaching schemes and competitions purely as a stepping-stone to turning professional.

Luckily, however, it is generally accepted among the better amateurs that nothing less than a Curtis Cup berth is an adequate qualification for the professional ranks, though it has to be said that they will not necessarily be able to stick with this ideal. For example, the golfer who is suddenly offered good sponsorship to play as a professional is hardly going to risk asking those sponsors if the money will still be there, say, in 18 months time when she has played in the Curtis Cup.

With this in mind, no-one can predict who will represent Great Britain and Ireland in the next match at Chattanooga. Suffice to say that there are plenty of great young players coming up, with pride of place going to Mhairi McKay, the 1992 British Girls' champion who, according to Tony Jacklin, exhibits much of the raw talent that Seve Ballesteros showed in his formative golfing years. The US side is also certain to have a very different look to it in 1994 - Vicki Goetze, for instance, will by then be playing the dollar-laden LPGA Tour.

It is not merely the possible personnel who will come under discussion at the various Curtis Cup meetings which will be taking place over the next few months. At the LGU's Centenary AGM the successful Great Britain and Ireland Captain, Liz Boatman said in her address that she felt it was time for an alteration in the format.

As things stand at the moment, only six players out of the eight are used at any one time. Boatman, who will be skippering again in 1994, did not suggest adding to the three morning foursomes, but she felt strongly that all eight players should be used in the afternoon singles.

It goes without saying that her views are coloured by what happened in the 1988 match at Royal St Georges when Ireland's Claire Hourihane was selected for the home side but never given a game. But the point she most likes to get across is that amateur golf is meant to be fun - and that any player who has done enough to get in the side deserves to be used.

Interestingly, the Americans have been calling for precisely the same changes in the Solheim Cup format, only in their case the request was born less of pity for those who

had been left out than the feeling that it was tantamount to an insult for players of such calibre to be asked to stand on the sidelines.

There is another common factor in the Curtis and Solheim Cups... Mickey Walker, who so successfully captained the Europeans in the Solheim Cup at Dalmahoy, was

chosen at the start of 1993 to follow Bernard Gallacher in working as a coach with the Great Britain and Ireland Curtis Cup squad.

'Bristol fashion' – the powerful action of England's 18 year-old Caroline Hall

Walker was delighted to be offered such an opportunity. As for the players, they could think of no-one better equipped to keep them on the right rails for Chattanooga.

The United States

4

1992 LPGA Tour Review

Number One in 1992 –
Dottie Mochrie has
become the player to
beat on the LPGA Tour

Was it the year of the twentysomethings? The year of the European Rookie perhaps? Or was it Canada's year? They, and much more, distinguished 1992: a year when Betsy King enjoyed a week to end all weeks; when Patty Sheehan had the summer to beat all summers and Dottie Mochrie, well, day-in day-out she was simply better than everyone else - statistically, financially and by just about every other yardstick you might care to mention. So whatever happened to the Pat Bradley - Beth Daniel show? And why didn't Amy Alcott add to her 29 wins and stroll into the Hall of Fame? The fact is, if not a wind, then a stiff breeze of change blew across the LPGA Tour in 1992. Although it may have yielded frosty repercussions for Daniel, Bradley, Alcott and one or two others, in the eyes of most it brought a thoroughly welcome 'freshness' to life on the Tour. It was a year that offered much, for there was even space for an end of year double-barrelled winning salute from Nancy Lopez.

Dottie Mochrie, who is profiled later in this chapter by Sonja Steptoe, was comfortably the golfer of the year in America. Just as Meg Mallon's LPGA - US Open winning double was the story of 1991 (Mallon, like Daniel and Bradley, surprised many by failing to win an event last year although she did finish runner-up three times) so Mochrie's emergence as the Tour's dominant force was surely the most significant happening of the 1992 season. Mochrie won four times - once more than anyone else - and claimed her first Major title after defeating Juli Inkster in

If Mochrie led the charge of the twentysomethings - during one spell in the first half of the season eight successive events were won by players aged under thirty - initially at least, both Danielle Ammaccapane and Brandie Burton chased hard on her heels. The stylish Ammaccapane

The price of success! Nancy Lopez remains as popular as ever

a playoff in the Nabisco Dinah Shore. (That event, along with the LPGA's other three Majors is reviewed separately.) In addition, Mochrie headed the Money List, collected the Rolex Player of the Year Award and for good measure picked up the Vare Trophy for achieving the lowest stroke average. In 1992 it seemed that only Dottie could be relied upon regularly to find that extra gear on Sunday afternoons.

won three tournaments and finished third on the Money List. In March she successfully defended her Standard Register/PING title at Moon Valley; a month later she won the Tour's richest event, the Centel Classic, scoring four rounds in the 60s and in June won the Lady Keystone Open. Burton, 1991's Rookie of the Year, was unlucky to win only once but a string of high finishes throughout the year confirmed her massive potential. Could Mochrie, Burton and Ammaccapane become the 'Big Three' of

(Far left) Michelle McGann has become one of the great characters — and stars — of the LPGA Tour.
(Left) There may have been more impressive wins in 1992, but Shelley Hamlin's victory was the greatest triumph.
(Opposite) Danielle Ammaccapane enjoyed her best ever season in 1992

American women's golf? Possibly, but several other young players made great strides in 1992, chief among whom were Donna Andrews, who came third in the US Open; Dana Lofland, winner of the Las Vegas International, and the colourful Michelle McGann who, according to the Tour statistics, is the longest driver on Tour and scores even more birdies than she buys new hats - and that is saying something.

Prior to 1992 Shelley Hamlin last won an LPGA Tour event in 1978; in July 1991 she was diagnosed as suffering from breast cancer and a mastectomy operation followed. In February, just six months after that operation, Hamlin won the Phar-Mor at Inverrary tournament shooting a final round

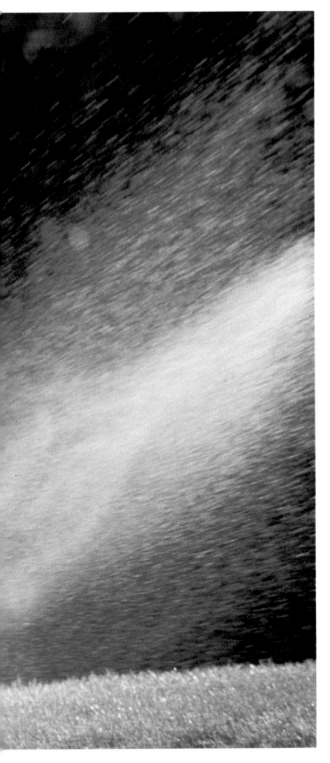

66. It was the most heart-warming story of the year: 'This victory is for all those women who have been through what I have been through', she said, adding, 'to let them know that they can still do whatever they want to do.'

There was plenty of joy up in British

Two of the all-time greats: (main picture) Beth Daniel, (left) Ayako Okamoto of Japan

Columbia too, during the early part of the season, for no fewer than three Canadians who hail from that state gained first tour successes, namely Lisa Walters, Dawn Coe and Jennifer Wyatt. Perhaps they should have been awarded a special prize as joint 'Rockies of the Year.'

If the twentysomethings seemed an irresistible force during the first half of the year, when spring turned to summer they came up against the golfing equivalent of the immovable object: a trio of thirtysomething superstars playing at their imperious best. Betsy King, Patty Sheehan and Juli Inkster hogged all the glory during the Mazda LPGA Championship and the Women's US Open. For good measure they also took most of the precious silverware that was on offer in between. Sheehan was especially brilliant,

Both Dana Lofland (right) and Sweden's Helen Alfredsson look less than happy – but both had spectacular seasons last year

winning three times in the space of five weeks. Colleen Walker (like Ammaccapane, Sheehan and King a three time winner in 1992) and Ayako Okamoto also did their bit for the reputation of the older generation and when towards the end of the year everybody's favourite, Nancy Lopez, scored back-to-back triumphs - her 45th and 46th LPGA Tour wins - it probably ended 'honours even' in the twenties versus thirties battle for hegemony.

Lopez's two victories in September also prevented the 1992 LPGA roll of winners from having a much more international look to it. In successive weeks the great heroine of American golf defeated Laura Davies of England and Jane Crafter of Australia in sudden-death playoffs. 'She's got a great future', Crafter joked at the prize presentation. As for Davies, it was her second playoff defeat of the season but then ample consolation awaited the popular big-hitter on the other side of the Atlantic.

Those who follow the fortunes of the LPGA Tour have become accustomed in recent years to seeing strong title challenges from Davies and Sweden's Lotte Neumann, both of whom of course have a US Open win to their name. Not many people were prepared however for the impact that Neumann's fellow Swede, Helen Alfredsson and Belgium's Florence Descampe would make in their debut seasons on Tour. Alfredsson won the Rookie of the Year prize and finished the year in 16th place on the Money List - ahead of such players as Bradley, Okamoto and Alcott - and indeed, Davies and Neumann. She didn't win a tournament, although came close on several occasions, while the more mercurial Descampe (24th on the Money List) did achieve the big breakthrough by winning the McCall's LPGA Classic at Stratton Mountain where she overtook and outplayed Dottie Mochrie on the final day.

Still learning and still improving, Alfredsson and Descampe are likely to make an even bigger impression on the LPGA Tour in 1993; moreover they will form part of an 18-strong European contingent now

No wins in 1992, but it will be a major surprise if Pat Bradley doesn't bounce back in 1993

carrying Tour Cards (the LPGA Tour's Final Qualifying school was a bit like a miniature rerun of the Solheim Cup) and a more cosmopolitan flavour to the Tour is assured in 1993. One shouldn't assume though that the Mochries, Burtons and Ammaccapanes are about to let the Europeans dash off with their newly won laurels. And you can also be sure that if there is one thing guaranteed to stir the competitive spirit in the Kings, Sheehans, Daniels and Bradleys even more than the challenge from the twentysomethings, it is the threat of a challenge from Europe's twentysomethings. Clearly, the 1993 season promises to be something special.

LPGA Majors

LPGA Majors

· ROLL OF HONOUR ·

NABISCO DINAH SHORE

1972	Jane Blalock
1973	Mickey Wright
1974	Jo Ann Prentice
1975	Sandra Palmer
1976	Judy Rankin
1977	Kathy Whitworth
1978	Sandra Post
1979	Sandra Post
1980	Donna Caponi
1981	Nancy Lopez
1982	Sally Little
1983*	Amy Alcott
1984	Juli Inkster
1985	Alice Miller
1986	Pat Bradley
1987	Betsy King
1988	Amy Alcott
1989	Juli Inkster
1990	Betsy King
1991	Amy Alcott
1992	Dottie Mochrie

*Designated a Major from 1983

MAZDA LPGA CHAMPIONSHIP

1955	Beverly Hanson
1956	Marlene Hagge
1957	Louise Suggs
1958	Mickey Wright
1959	Betsy Rawls
1960	Mickey Wright
1961	Mickey Wright
1962	Judy Kimball
1963	Mickey Wright
1964	Mary Mills
1965	Sandra Haynie
1966	Gloria Ehret
1967	Kathy Whitworth
1968	Sandra Post
1969	Betsy Rawls
1970	Shirley Englehorn
1971	Kathy Whitworth
1972	Kathy Ahern
1973	Mary Mills
1974	Sandra Haynie
1975	Kathy Whitworth
1976	Betty Burfeindt
1977	Chako Higuchi
1978	Nancy Lopez
1979	Donna Caponi
1980	Sally Little
1981	Donna Caponi
1982	Jan Stephenson
1983	Patty Sheehan
1984	Patty Sheehan
1985	Nancy Lopez
1986	Pat Bradley
1987	Jane Geddes
1988	Sherri Turner
1989	Nancy Lopez
1990	Beth Daniel
1991	Meg Mallon
1992	Betsy King

DU MAURIER LTD. CLASSIC

1973	Jocelyne Bourassa
1974	Carole Jo Callison
1975	JoAnne Carner
1976	Donna Caponi
1977	Judy Rankin
1978	JoAnne Carner
1979*	Amy Alcott
1980	Pat Bradley
1981	Jan Stephenson
1982	Sandra Haynie
1983	Hollis Stacy
1984	Juli Inkster
1985	Pat Bradley
1986	Pat Bradley
1987	Jody Rosenthal
1988	Sally Little
1989	Tammie Green
1990	Cathy Johnston
1991	Nancy Scranton
1992	Sherri Steinhauer

*Designated a Major from 1979

US OPEN

1946	Patty Berg
1947	Betty Jameson
1948	Babe Zaharias
1949	Louise Suggs
1950	Babe Zaharias
1951	Betsy Rawls
1952	Louise Suggs
1953	Betsy Rawls
1954	Babe Zaharias
1955	Fay Crocker

1956	Kathy Cornelius
1957	Betsy Rawls
1958	Mickey Wright
1959	Mickey Wright
1960	Betsy Rawls
1961	Mickey Wright
1962	Murle Lindstrom
1963	Mary Mills
1964	Mickey Wright
1965	Carol Mann
1966	Sandra Spuzich
1967	Catherine Lacoste
1968	Susie Berning
1969	Donna Caponi
1970	Donna Caponi
1971	JoAnne Gunderson Carner
1972	Susie Berning
1973	Susie Berning
1974	Sandra Haynie
1975	Sandra Palmer
1976	JoAnne Gunderson Carner
1977	Hollis Stacy
1978	Hollis Stacy
1979	Jerilyn Britz
1980	Amy Alcott
1981	Pat Bradley
1982	Janet Alex
1983	Jan Stephenson
1984	Hollis Stacy
1985	Kathy Baker
1986	Jane Geddes
1987	Laura Davies
1988	Liselotte Neumann
1989	Betsy King
1990	Betsy King
1991	Meg Mallon
1992	Patty Sheehan

*Betsy King's stunning win in the
1992 Mazda LPGA Championship
was her fifth Major success*

1992 LPGA Majors

Can you realistically measure greatness in golf or is it merely a matter of opinion? In the women's game there are at least two standards that provide ammunition for those who care to judge and debate. The first is membership of the LPGA's Hall of Fame - a club so exclusive it once earned the remark 'more people have climbed to the summit of Mount Everest than there are members of the LPGA Hall of Fame.' The second benchmark is the winning of Major titles - not as difficult to achieve, although the air can become incredibly rarefied in the process. There are presently four such championships in women's golf (although European tour members might argue that the British Open now represents a fifth). Of course, not every Major is won by a 'great' player but the important point is that in order to become recognised as being 'great' it seems one must win one, and preferably several, of these events.

This is why her playoff victory in the 1992 Nabisco Dinah Shore meant so much to Dottie Mochrie, and doubtless contributed immensely to her going on to attain - dare one say it - the heights of

Two stars and a setting sun – Dottie Mochrie wins the Dinah Shore at Mission Hills

'greatness' last season. It also explains why Patty Sheehan will probably cherish 1992 above all others in her illustrious career and, given the parenthesised comment above, it is worth remembering that at Woburn in September she became the first golfer ever to achieve the women's US - British Open could justifiably describe her success in *Golf World* as, 'probably the best four days of golf any woman has ever played'. Finally, the 'Majors factor' is the reason why Sherri Steinhauer's career has been elevated to another level following her unexpected, but very popular, triumph in the LPGA's final

Michelle McGann putts as Sherri Steinhauer looks on at Mission Hills

double in the same calendar year. Surely only a Major victory could have induced Betsy King to high-five her way down an 18th fairway and it was because her magnificent performance in May last year happened in one of the 'big four' events that leading journalist Geoff Russell

Major of the season, Canada's du Maurier Classic. Sherri may not be a 'great' player yet but she has at least now laid the necessary foundations.

So, the spectacular setting of Mission Hills, Palm Springs (superbly captured by Bob Ewell's photograph opposite and on pages 48-49) is where Dottie Mochrie chose

Juli Inkster (right) is about to lose the first of two Major playoffs in 1992

to join the Major league. Maybe 'chose' is a bit strong given that for much of the weekend it looked as if Juli Inkster was heading towards her third Dinah Shore title in nine years. Rounds of 72-68-68 had given the Californian a slender lead going into the final round, and for 17 holes on Sunday she held on to it. But all day long, Inkster had had Mochrie and her close friend and rival, Patty Sheehan breathing down her neck. When the three came to the par five 18th tee, Mochrie was fired-up in the way only someone whose maiden name is Pepper can be - thanks in no small part to the spectator who had dared to yell 'loser' when she left a holeable birdie putt short on the 71st hole - while Sheehan had just birdied each of the last three holes: Inkster was under pressure! Some 15 minutes later Sheehan had bogied, Inkster had parred (missing a five foot putt for the title) and Mochrie had made a classic drive-position-pitch-three foot putt-birdie.

Dottie, who finished second in the Dinah Shore in 1991, had forced a playoff and with the impetus very firmly with her, went on to capture the title at the first sudden-death hole. Given the nature of both win and winner there were not surprisingly emotional scenes, although no repeat of the previous year when Amy Alcott dived into the greenside lake taking the sprightly Dinah Shore with her. The victory was to prove the making of Mochrie.

Mission Hills is widely acknowledged as one of the most demanding layouts that the players face on tour; similarly regarded is Bethesda, current home of the year's second Major, the Mazda LPGA Championship. It is often remarked how usually 'the cream rises to the top' when these toughest tests are confronted, and a glance at the names heading the list of finishers in both the '92 Dinah Shore and LPGA events (see page 71) confirms as much. On closer inspection, however, only one name stands out among the LPGA scores, that of Betsy King, who committed the exact opposite of regicide on the rest of the field. She murdered the reputation of Bethesda too, storming around the Maryland course in rounds of 68-66-67-66 for an eleven stroke victory. She established numerous scoring records in the process - and not just for the championship itself: her 267 total was the lowest in the

*Bethesda was
beautifully prepared
for the '92 LPGA
Championship — but no
player was prepared
for Betsy King*

P i n g   W o m e n ' s   G o l f   Y e a r

Tour's history and she became the first player to break 70 in all four rounds of an LPGA Major; not since the legendary 'Babe' Zaharias won the 1954 US Open by 12 had a player so dominated a Major championship - and the fields of course were a great deal weaker in the 1950s.

It was an extraordinary performance in many ways. For one thing, King's early season form had been decidedly unimpressive and it took her 29 tournament rounds before she scored in the 60s. As mentioned, Bethesda is the type of course that 'takes no prisoners': it is very tight

The headline-maker of 1991: Meg Mallon surrendered her LPGA title to Betsy King and her US Open crown to Patty Sheehan

with a dense spread of trees bordering almost every fairway, and the weather was both foggy and damp making the course play its full length. During the entire championship King only dropped two shots - both in the second round - and her last 47 holes comprised 34 pars and 13 birdies.

From soggy Bethesda to Soakmont. Or rather Oakmont. 'In all my years in women's professional golf, I cannot recall a single tournament, much less a Major in which Mother Nature had a bigger say', so wrote Sandra Haynie in *Golf for Women* magazine. Rain and thunder stoppages were

There were others who played well that week in May, notably 25-year-old rookie Karen Noble, whose brilliant fourth round 65 earned her a share of second place alongside 53-year-old Hall of Famer, JoAnne Carner and Sweden's Lotte Neumann. Another Swede, Helen Alfredsson finished joint fifth, but there was only ever one winner. 'When Betsy gets hot, she just goes out and whips our butts', commented Carner in her own inimitable way. Or, as John Stewart put it in *Golfweek*, 'Binoculars were needed to bring in the rest of the field.'

the norm at Oakmont last year, yet the 47th US Women's Open was a very special one. There were two main reasons: firstly, the quality of the course and secondly, the quality of the champion. Despite the downpours, Oakmont was a big hit with the players. That comment was not intended as a pun but at 6312 yards, par 71, and in such conditions, it probably played longer than any course in the championship's history. Certainly the shorter hitters in the field found several of the par fours to be out of reach in two

Patty Sheehan with the US Open trophy and (left) Pam Wright

shots. It was a big hit simply because it presented such a magnificent, not to mention historic, challenge. Oakmont is one of the greatest courses in the world and included among its six (men's) US Open champions are

An airborne Patty Sheehan is on her way to a first US Open title

Board we can now add the name of Patty Sheehan, one of the all-time greats of women's golf.

Britain's Pam Wright, a European Solheim Cup player and the 1989 LPGA Rookie of the Year, led the championship after 36 holes before falling away in the final

arguably the two greatest professional golfers of all time - Ben Hogan and Jack Nicklaus - and among its four US Amateur champions, Bobby Jones, unquestionably the finest amateur golfer. To the Oakmont Honours

two rounds. Another player who made her mark at Oakmont was 24-year-old Donna Andrews who finished a very commendable third, one place ahead of the defending champion, Meg Mallon. But if the LPGA

Championship was all about one player, the US Open was essentially a tale of two players, Juli Inkster and Patty Sheehan and, of course, ultimately (if there's any truth in the old saying that nobody remembers who came second), about one player.

As at Mission Hills in the opening Major of the year, it looked for much of the final day as if Inkster would be that player, but, once again, somebody was ominously perched on her shoulder as she approached the closing stretch. This time though, it was just Sheehan who could deny her. The two players - both seeking a first US Open title - had begun the day three shots ahead of the field and it developed into a classic head-to-head confrontation. When Sheehan three putted the 16th green on Sunday she found herself two behind with two to play. As determined a player as she is, she must have been thinking that a fourth US Open runner-up finish was destined to be her fate. Both drove safely at the 71st hole... then the sirens sounded - yet another storm stoppage to add to the several that had occurred over the first four days.

The delay lasted for one hour 45 minutes and on resumption Sheehan played probably the two most sensational and significant holes of her life. Inkster did little wrong, parring those two holes, but her former college team-mate birdied them both - the 17th from 10 feet and then, after watching Inkster miss a putt for the title from 20 feet, she rammed home a 16 footer for a second birdie to tie. In Monday's 18 hole playoff Sheehan picked up where she left off by birdieing the 1st and thereafter was never caught, eventually winning with a 72 to Inkster's 74.

In the US Open at Atlanta in 1990 Sheehan had frittered away a nine stroke lead over the final 27 holes. Naturally the experience wounded her deeply, but at Oakmont any lingering scars were instantly healed. All it needed was a clap of thunder and a touch of genius. If not exactly poles apart, Missouri and

Sherri Steinhauer wins the final LPGA Major of the year

Manitoba are many miles from one another; in the same week, on the outskirts of St Louis and Winnipeg, the men's and ladies' games staged their fourth and final Major championships of the year.

Champion of St Charles: Sherri Steinhauer poses
with the Du Maurier trophy
(Photo courtesy of Don Vickery/du Maurier Ltd Golf Library)

The USPGA and the du Maurier Classic are, it is probably fair to say, the least glamorous of the Major championships - not that 'glamour' itself holds weight - but both titles are eagerly sought after and over the years have been won by great champions. The du Maurier, for instance (which is always held in Canada), has been won by three Hall of Famers: JoAnne Carner (twice), Sandra Haynie and Pat Bradley (three times). In recent years, however surprise winners have emerged, and 1992 followed this trend.

At the St Charles Golf Club, 29-year-old Sherri Steinhauer picked the perfect week to win her first Tour event. Yes, first Tour event - never mind first Major championship. She achieved it with the help of two 67s, one in the first round and another in the third, after which she led the field, and then, showing great composure, stayed in front all the way to the finishing line. She was pursued, if not seriously pressed, to the end by Judy Dickinson, who started the final day just a stroke behind Steinhauer and finished two behind. In third place, just a stroke back of Dickinson and finishing strongly with a 68, was guess who - Juli Inkster. And you can be sure that it is no consolation whatsoever for Juli that she finished the year with the best aggregate total for the four Majors. If ever there was an 'if only' season, it was Inkster's in 1992.

With Canadian golfers enjoying such a fine year on the LPGA Tour - three players, Lisa Walters, Dawn Coe and Jennifer Wyatt had won tournaments - a strong 'home' challenge had been anticipated at St Charles. But it never materialised, and so Sherri, a slender, smiling vision in turquoise on Sunday, slipped quietly into the world of Major championship winners.

1992 · LPGA Majors

March 26-29
Nabisco Dinah Shore
MISSION HILLS COUNTRY CLUB,
RANCHO MIRAGE, CA

* Dottie Mochrie	69	71	70	69	279	$105000
Juli Inkster	72	68	68	71	279	65165
Brandie Burton	70	72	71	68	281	42269
Patty Sheehan	71	69	69	72	281	42269
Meg Mallon	73	69	72	68	282	29940
Sherri Steinhauer	72	73	69	70	284	22719
Dale Eggeling	67	78	69	70	284	22719
Kris Tschetter	73	71	73	68	285	15778
Pamela Wright	74	71	71	69	285	15778
Beth Daniel	70	68	76	71	285	15778
Elaine Crosby	72	70	73	71	286	11335
Ayako Okamoto	71	71	72	72	286	11335
Muffin Spencer-Devlin	73	69	71	73	286	11335
Jan Stephenson	72	72	68	74	286	11335
Tammie Green	70	70	74	73	287	9574
Chris Johnson	71	71	75	71	288	8517
JoAnne Carner	70	72	75	71	288	8517
Jane Geddes	75	68	73	72	288	8517
Pat Bradley	73	71	69	75	288	8517

* Mochrie won playoff at first extra hole

July 23-26
US Women's Open Championship
OAKMONT COUNTRY CLUB, OAKMONT, PA

* Patty Sheehan	69	72	70	69	280	$130000
Juli Inkster	72	68	71	69	280	65000
Donna Andrews	69	73	72	70	284	38830
Meg Mallon	73	72	72	70	287	28336
Dawn Coe	71	71	72	74	288	22295
Dottie Mochrie	70	74	72	73	289	17472
Michelle McGann	72	73	70	74	289	17472
Gail Graham	72	71	71	75	289	17472
Jane Geddes	73	70	78	70	291	13372
Tammie Green	73	75	70	73	291	13372
Pamela Wright	70	69	76	76	291	13372
Mitzi Edge	73	74	72	73	292	11731
Amy Alcott	76	74	73	70	293	10887
Helen Alfredsson	71	79	72	71	293	10887
Liselotte Neumann	76	72	72	74	294	10111
Nancy Lopez	75	76	71	73	295	8674
Suzanne Strudwick	75	73	73	74	295	8674
Michelle Estill	74	74	73	74	295	8674
Ok-Hee Ku	73	74	74	74	295	8674
Betsy King	74	73	73	75	295	8674

* Sheehan won 18 hole playoff by 72 to 74

May 11-17
Mazda LPGA Championship
BETHESDA COUNTRY CLUB, BETHESDA, MD

Betsy King	68	66	67	66	267	$150000
Karen Noble	73	70	70	65	278	71287
Liselotte Neumann	71	68	70	69	278	71287
JoAnne Carner	71	66	70	71	278	71287
Dottie Mochrie	71	73	68	67	279	38998
Helen Alfredsson	69	69	68	73	279	38998
Patty Sheehan	71	70	69	70	280	27928
Alice Ritzman	68	71	71	70	280	27928
Juli Inkster	70	71	66	74	281	23651
Brandie Burton	68	73	70	71	282	20128
Amy Alcott	69	69	73	71	282	20128
Shelley Hamlin	72	72	70	69	283	16605
Donna Andrews	68	75	68	72	283	16605
Jan Stephenson	69	71	70	73	283	16605
Ayako Okamoto	71	70	75	68	284	13754
Pat Bradley	70	71	74	69	284	13754

August 13-16
Du Maurier Ltd Classic
ST CHARLES COUNTRY CLUB, WINNIPEG, CANADA

Sherri Steinhauer	67	73	67	70	277	$105000
Judy Dickinson	70	71	67	71	279	65165
Juli Inkster	70	69	73	68	280	47553
Ellie Gibson	71	73	74	65	283	36985
Shelley Hamlin	74	68	75	67	284	29940
Tina Barrett	74	71	70	70	285	17269
Donna Andrews	73	69	72	71	285	17269
Barb Mucha	71	71	72	71	285	17269
Kristi Albers	70	68	75	72	285	17269
Caroline Keggi	73	71	68	73	285	17269
Florence Descampe	71	71	70	73	285	17269
Tammie Green	70	71	70	74	285	17269
Pamela Wright	72	74	73	67	286	9848
Cindy Rarick	70	76	73	67	286	9848
Patty Sheehan	70	74	72	70	286	9848
Meg Mallon	67	73	72	74	286	9848

1992 LPGA Tour Results

January 30 - February 2
OLDSMOBILE LPGA CLASSIC
WYCLIFFE GOLF AND COUNTRY CLUB,
LAKE WORTH, FL

* Colleen Walker	71	73	67	68	279	$60000
Dawn Coe	67	73	69	70	279	37237
Beth Daniel	66	71	73	70	280	27173
Katie Peterson-Parker	73	71	71	66	281	19121
Deb Richard	70	70	71	70	281	19121
Helen Alfredsson	66	71	72	73	282	14089
Jane Geddes	73	73	68	69	283	9583
Patty Sheehan	70	72	71	70	283	9583
Shelley Hamlin	70	74	68	71	283	9583
Rosie Jones	68	71	72	72	283	9583
Pat Bradley	70	67	72	74	283	9583

February 7-9
PHAR-MOR AT INVERRARY
INVERRARY COUNTRY CLUB & RESORT,
FT. LAUDERDALE, FL

Shelley Hamlin	72	68	66	206	$75000
Brandie Burton	70	68	69	207	35643
Dana Lofland	70	66	71	207	35643
JoAnne Carner	69	67	71	207	35643
Pat Bradley	69	70	69	208	21386
Rosie Jones	71	69	69	209	16228
Danielle Ammaccapane	70	68	71	209	16228
Colleen Walker	70	73	67	210	11825
Becky Pearson	72	67	71	210	11825
Tammie Green	71	68	71	210	11825

February 20-22
ITOKI HAWAIIAN OPEN
KO OLINA GOLF CLUB, EWA BEACH, OAHU, HAWAII

Lisa Walters	72	71	65	208	$60000
Kristi Albers	73	68	68	209	32205
Michele M Berteotti	71	67	71	209	32205
Dottie Mochrie	74	71	65	210	19121

Michelle McGann	71	67	72	210	19121
Karen Davies	75	68	69	212	14089
Patty Sheehan	72	72	69	213	10600
Karen Noble	73	69	71	213	10600
Pat Bradley	69	73	71	213	10600

February 26-29
KEMPER OPEN
WAILEA GOLF CLUB, KIHEI, MAUI, HAWAII

Dawn Coe	68	70	69	68	275	$75000
Dottie Mochrie	67	74	71	64	276	46546
Michele M Berteotti	66	72	70	69	277	33966
Dana Lofland	71	68	73	66	278	26418
Michelle McGann	71	67	72	69	279	19499
Cindy Rarick	73	65	70	71	279	19499
Brandie Burton	70	71	71	68	280	13963
Tammie Green	71	70	70	69	280	13963
Meg Mallon	73	70	70	68	281	10651
Betsy King	71	70	70	70	281	10651
Mitzi Edge	70	71	70	70	281	10651

Lisa Walters, one of Canada's three first-time winners

March 5-8
INAMORI CLASSIC
STONERIDGE COUNTRY CLUB, POWAY, CA

Judy Dickinson	69	69	69	70	277	$63750
Meg Mallon	70	68	74	67	279	39564
Debbie Massey	73	72	69	70	284	23168
Cindy Figg-Currier	75	68	70	71	284	23168
Elaine Crosby	70	68	72	74	284	23168
Helen Alfredsson	70	72	74	69	285	14970
Ok-Hee Ku	75	68	71	72	286	12617
Tina Barrett	73	72	72	70	287	10051
Nina Foust	72	71	74	70	287	10051
Michelle Mackall	74	67	74	72	287	10051

March 12-15
PING/WELCH'S CHAMPIONSHIP
RANDOLPH PARK NORTH, TUCSON, AZ

Brandie Burton	71	69	69	68	277	$60000
Dale Eggeling	69	70	70	69	278	32205
Beth Daniel	70	68	67	73	278	32205
Jill Briles-Hinton	75	66	72	67	280	21134
Kate Golden	72	70	71	68	281	14357
Anne Marie Palli	69	71	71	70	281	14357
Pat Bradley	67	76	66	72	281	14357
Alice Ritzman	71	73	67	72	283	10466
Ayako Okamoto	73	72	68	71	284	8520
Michelle McGann	74	70	69	71	284	8520
Colleen Walker	71	71	69	73	284	8520

March 19-22
STANDARD REGISTER PING
MOON VALLEY COUNTRY CLUB, PHOENIX, AZ

Danielle Ammaccapane	72	69	69	69	279	$82500
Kristi Albers	73	69	71	68	281	51201
Dawn Coe	72	71	72	67	282	33211
Marta Figueras-Dotti	72	67	72	71	282	33211
Alice Ritzman	72	71	72	69	284	23524
Jane Geddes	74	71	72	68	285	16697
Martha Nause	71	73	72	69	285	16697
Meg Mallon	69	74	71	71	285	16697
Pat Bradley	72	74	71	69	286	13008
Brandie Burton	77	69	71	70	287	10628
Deb Richard	72	73	71	71	287	10628
Nancy Scranton	69	73	73	72	287	10628

* denotes winner after playoff

March 26-29
NABISCO DINAH SHORE
MISSION HILLS COUNTRY CLUB,
RANCHO MIRAGE, CA

(See page 71)

Moon Valley's double champion, Danielle Ammaccapane

April 3-5
LAS VEGAS LPGA INTERNATIONAL
DESERT INN COUNTRY CLUB, LAS VEGAS, NV

Dana Lofland	70	71	71	212	$67500
Missie Berteotti	73	73	68	214	32078
Judy Dickinson	69	73	72	214	32078
Beth Daniel	69	73	72	214	32078
Ok-Hee Ku	73	75	67	215	16152
Gina Hull	73	71	71	215	16152
Florence Descampe	67	74	74	215	16152
Stephanie Farwig	77	71	68	216	9321
Carolyn Hill	74	72	70	216	9321
Allison Finney	72	74	70	216	9321
Jan Stephenson	70	75	71	216	9321
Amy Alcott	71	70	75	216	9321
Jane Geddes	69	72	75	216	9321

April 16-19
SEGA CHAMPIONSHIP
EAGLE'S LANDING COUNTRY CLUB
STOCKBRIDGE, GA

Dottie Mochrie	70	69	68	70	277	$90000
Danielle Ammaccapane	71	70	67	70	278	55855
Sherri Steinhauer	72	71	68	68	279	32708
Helen Alfredsson	71	68	71	69	279	32708
Beth Daniel	68	71	69	71	279	32708
Meg Mallon	75	69	68	68	280	19473
Deb Richard	67	67	71	75	280	19473
Elaine Crosby	71	67	71	72	281	15700
Juli Inkster	73	71	68	71	283	13435
Brandie Burton	70	70	72	71	283	13435
Mitzi Edge	69	74	66	75	284	11473
Jody Anschutz	70	71	72	72	285	10567

April 24-26
SARA LEE CLASSIC
HERMITAGE GOLF COURSE, OLD HICKORY, TN

* Maggie Will	71	69	67	207	$78750
Amy Benz	67	77	63	207	42268
Brandie Burton	68	69	70	207	42268
Dawn Coe	67	70	71	208	22895
Tina Barrett	66	71	71	208	22895
Dana Lofland	65	71	72	208	22895
Carolyn Hill	66	75	68	209	15586
Kathy Postlewait	70	73	67	210	11306
Becky Pearson	73	69	68	210	11306

Angie Ridgeway	66	75	69	210	11306
Dottie Mochrie	69	71	70	210	11306
Lauri Merten	69	71	70	210	11306

April 30-May 3
CENTEL CLASSIC
KILLEARN COUNTRY CLUB, TALLAHASSEE, FL

Danielle Ammaccapane	69	68	69	69	275	$180000
Colleen Walker	64	74	68	70	276	85544
Michelle Estill	66	71	69	70	276	85544
Liselotte Neumann	68	70	67	71	276	85544
Lori Garbacz	71	69	72	67	279	43073
Meg Mallon	68	71	70	70	279	43073
Brandie Burton	71	69	68	71	279	43073
Alice Ritzman	67	71	71	71	280	31400
Donna Andrews	71	71	71	68	281	23550
Pat Bradley	70	69	73	69	281	23550
Missie Berteotti	68	71	71	71	281	23550
Betsy King	73	67	68	73	281	23550
Dottie Mochrie	69	70	68	74	281	23550
Martha Nause	74	66	72	70	282	17511
Donna White	70	70	71	71	282	17511
Lynn Connelly	69	70	72	71	282	17511

May 8-10
CRESTAR-FARM FRESH CLASSIC
GREENBRIER COUNTRY CLUB, CHESAPEAKE, VA

Jennifer Wyatt	70	68	70	208	$63750
Donna Andrews	70	67	73	210	39564
Ayako Okamoto	68	70	73	211	28871
Barb Bunkowsky	71	71	72	214	18534
Michelle McGann	68	72	74	214	18534
Dana Lofland	68	69	77	214	18534
Caroline Pierce	72	68	75	215	11868
Juli Inkster	71	68	76	215	11868
Betsy King	70	73	73	216	9053
Tani Tatum	71	71	74	216	9053
Dale Eggeling	71	69	76	216	9053

May 11-17
MAZDA LPGA CHAMPIONSHIP
BETHESDA COUNTRY CLUB, BETHESDA, MD

(See page 71)

LPGA CORNING CLASSIC

May 21-24

CORNING COUNTRY CLUB, CORNING, NY

Colleen Walker	65	70	69	72	276	$67500
Alice Miller	68	74	68	71	281	36230
Beth Daniel	73	68	69	71	281	36230

Rosie Jones	71	70	69	72	282	23776
Mitzi Edge	72	70	66	75	283	19247
Kelly Robbins	73	68	72	71	284	13661
Brandie Burton	70	70	73	71	284	13661
JoAnne Carner	69	71	67	77	284	13661
Lisa Walters	72	73	70	70	285	10642
Patty Sheehan	72	72	72	70	286	8118
Betsy King	73	70	72	71	286	8118
Kathy Postlewait	73	70	68	75	286	8118
Tara Fleming	73	68	70	75	286	8118
Sherri Steinhauer	72	67	72	75	286	8118

May 28-31

OLDSMOBILE CLASSIC

WALNUT HILLS COUNTRY CLUB, EAST LANSING, MI

Barb Mucha	70	70	65	71	276	$75000
Dottie Mochrie	67	70	73	67	277	46546
Deb Richard	72	64	69	73	278	33966
Beth Daniel	73	66	73	67	279	26418
Chris Johnson	73	67	68	72	280	19499
Nancy Lopez	72	65	71	72	280	19499
Brandie Burton	74	69	69	69	281	13963
Jane Geddes	71	71	65	74	281	13963
Mary Murphy	72	67	76	67	282	10207
Kelly Robbins	73	70	69	70	282	10207
Ayako Okamoto	69	71	71	71	282	10207
Judy Dickinson	66	71	71	74	282	10207

June 4-7

McDONALD'S CHAMPIONSHIP

DUPONT COUNTRY CLUB, WILMINGTON, DE

Ayako Okamoto	67	69	69	205	$112500
Pat Bradley	72	70	66	208	53465
Deb Richard	68	70	70	208	53465
Brandie Burton	73	63	72	208	53465
Judy Dickinson	70	68	71	209	32079
Jane Geddes	77	65	68	210	24342
Dottie Mochrie	71	70	69	210	24342
Michelle McGann	74	69	68	211	16888
Colleen Walker	72	70	69	211	16888
Nancy Scranton	70	72	69	211	16888
Nancy Lopez	67	73	71	211	16888
Helen Alfredsson	72	71	69	212	11699
Kim Shipman	71	72	69	212	11699
Danielle Ammaccapane	72	70	70	212	11699
Jane Crafter	72	69	71	212	11699
Caroline Keggi	70	70	72	212	11699

Colleen Walker collected three LPGA titles in 1992

Ping Women's Golf Year

SHOPRITE LPGA CLASSIC

June 12-14

GREATE BAY RESORT & COUNTRY CLUB
SOMERS POINT, NJ

* Anne Marie Palli	69	69	69	207	$60000
Laura Davies	71	67	69	207	37237
Betsy King	71	68	69	208	27173
Pearl Sinn	71	72	66	209	19121
Ayako Okamoto	70	69	70	209	19121
Meg Mallon	70	70	70	210	12982
Dana Lofland	70	69	71	210	12982
Amy Alcott	70	72	69	211	9007
Caroline Keggi	73	67	71	211	9007
Lauri Merten	71	69	71	211	9007
Hiromi Kobayashi	66	73	72	211	9007
Jennifer Wyatt	74	71	68	213	7044

LADY KEYSTONE OPEN

June 19-21

HERSHEY COUNTRY CLUB, HERSHEY, PA

Danielle Ammaccapane	68	71	69	208	$60000
Muffin Spencer-Devlin	69	73	68	210	28514
Lori West	69	71	70	210	28514
Nancy Lopez	70	67	73	210	28514
Laurel Kean	66	75	71	212	15598
Hollis Stacy	71	67	74	212	15598
Michelle Mackall	73	71	69	213	11875
Donna Andrews	70	72	73	215	9460
Colleen Walker	70	72	73	215	9460
Rosie Jones	70	71	74	215	9460
Helen Alfredsson	74	71	71	216	7148
Gina Hull	71	72	73	216	7148
Denise Baldwin	70	73	73	216	7148

ROCHESTER INTERNATIONAL

June 25-28

LOCUST HILL COUNTRY CLUB, PITTSFORD, NY

Patty Sheehan	70	65	63	71	269	$60000
Nancy Lopez	66	71	73	68	278	37237
Jane Crafter	73	68	69	69	279	27173
Hollis Stacy	73	69	69	68	280	21134
Danielle Ammaccapane	69	71	73	68	281	15598
Michelle McGann	67	70	70	74	281	15598
Jennifer Wyatt	71	70	73	69	283	11170
Sherri Steinhauer	72	68	73	70	283	11170
Dawn Coe	71	69	70	74	284	9460

JAMIE FARR TOLEDO CLASSIC

July 3-5

HIGHLAND MEADOWS GOLF CLUB, SYLVANIA, OH

Patty Sheehan	70	73	66	209	$60000
Brandie Burton	70	71	69	210	25663
Heather Drew	70	70	70	210	25663
Tammie Green	70	68	72	210	25663
Deb Richard	71	66	73	210	25663
Hollis Stacy	72	68	71	211	12982
Pamela Wright	69	71	71	211	12982
Vicki Fergon	65	77	70	212	8614
JoAnne Carner	70	71	71	212	8614
Janice Gibson	67	74	71	212	8614
Marta Figueras-Dotti	69	70	73	212	8614
Meg Mallon	68	70	74	212	8614

THE PHAR-MOR IN YOUNGSTOWN

SQUAW CREEK COUNTRY CLUB, VIENNA, OH

* Betsy King	71	67	71	209	$75000
Beth Daniel	70	69	70	209	35643
Donna Andrews	70	69	70	209	35643
Meg Mallon	69	69	71	209	35643
Sherri Steinhauer	74	68	68	210	16731
Juli Inkster	74	68	68	210	16731
Dottie Mochrie	70	69	71	210	16731
Katie Peterson-Parker	70	68	72	210	16731
Pat Bradley	72	71	68	211	10654
Nancy Lopez	69	71	71	211	10654
Denise Baldwin	68	71	72	211	10654

JAL BIG APPLE CLASSIC

July 16-19

WYKAGYL COUNTRY CLUB, NEW ROCHELLE, NY

Juli Inkster	66	64	69	74	273	$75000
Nancy Lopez	67	70	71	67	275	46546
Joan Pitcock	72	67	69	70	278	33966
Meg Mallon	73	70	68	69	280	21805
Tammie Green	68	73	69	70	280	21805
Dana Lofland	70	68	72	70	280	21805
Betsy King	70	71	71	69	281	13963
Jane Geddes	69	69	69	74	281	13963

US WOMEN'S OPEN CHAMPIONSHIP

July 23-26

OAKMONT COUNTRY CLUB, OAKMONT, PA

(See page 71)

July 30-August 2
WELCH'S CLASSIC
BLUE HILL COUNTRY CLUB, CANTON, MA

Dottie Mochrie	72	67	69	70	278	$63750
Stephanie Farwig	68	73	76	64	281	39564
Sherri Steinhauer	70	68	70	74	282	28871
Florence Descampe	68	70	72	75	285	22455
Juli Inkster	70	72	76	68	286	13387
Danielle Ammaccapane	73	70	73	70	286	13387
Nancy Lopez	71	71	74	70	286	13387
Susie Redman	74	72	69	71	286	13387
Alice Ritzman	70	70	74	72	286	13387
Cindy Rarick	75	73	73	66	287	8207
Dana Lofland	72	71	72	72	287	8207
Amy Alcott	72	70	73	72	287	8207

August 6-9
McCALL'S LPGA CLASSIC
AT STRATTON MOUNTAIN
STRATTON MOUNTAIN COUNTRY CLUB
STRATTON MOUNTAIN, VT

Florence Descampe	73	69	69	67	278	$75000
Dottie Mochrie	68	70	71	71	280	46546
Sarah McGuire	70	73	72	67	282	22845
Caroline Keggi	72	70	71	69	282	22845
Nina Foust	72	68	73	69	282	22845
Betsy King	70	66	74	72	282	22845
Cindy Rarick	71	72	66	73	282	22845
Kris Tschetter	71	72	71	69	283	10786
Laura Davies	73	68	73	69	283	10786
Susie Redman	71	71	71	70	283	10786
Robin Walton	70	70	73	70	283	10786
Rosie Jones	72	69	69	73	283	10786
Missie Berteotti	72	71	71	70	284	8097
Patty Sheehan	71	72	70	71	284	8097

August 13-16
DU MAURIER LTD CLASSIC
ST CHARLES COUNTRY CLUB, WINNIPEG, CANADA

(See page 71)

Rookie with a golden glow:
Belgian star Florence Descampe
won at Stratton Mountain, so
beating her friend and rival Helen
Alfredsson to a first LPGA title

August 21-23
NORTHGATE COMPUTER CLASSIC
EDINBURGH USA GOLF COURSE,
BROOKLYN PARK, MN

Kris Tschetter	69	69	73	211	$63750
Deb Richard	69	70	75	214	39564
Betsy King	69	76	71	216	25663
Judy Dickinson	67	76	73	216	25663
Helen Alfredsson	69	77	71	217	14221
Danielle Ammaccapane	69	73	75	217	14221
Dottie Mochrie	68	74	75	217	14221
Laura Baugh	71	70	76	217	14221
Cindy Rarick	74	71	73	218	9516
Juli Inkster	71	73	74	218	9516

August 27-30
SUN-TIMES CHALLENGE
WHITE EAGLE GOLF CLUB, NAPERVILLE, IL

* Dottie Mochrie	71	72	73	216	$67500
Judy Dickinson	73	71	72	216	36230
Beth Daniel	71	72	73	216	36230
Caroline Keggi	73	71	74	218	23776
Barb Bunkowsky	74	70	75	219	19247
Julie Larsen	76	69	75	220	15850
Meg Mallon	74	74	73	221	13360
Sally Little	77	70	75	222	11208
Val Skinner	74	70	78	222	11208

September 5-7
RAIL CHARITY GOLF CLASSIC
RAIL GOLF CLUB, SPRINGFIELD, IL

* Nancy Lopez	67	68	64	199	$67500
Laura Davies	68	64	67	199	41891
Florence Descampe	67	67	66	200	30569
Missie Berteotti	70	66	66	202	18058
Donna Andrews	67	67	68	202	18058
Betsy King	67	66	69	202	18058
Michelle McGann	66	67	69	202	18058
Angie Ridgeway	65	72	67	204	11208
Rosie Jones	65	68	71	204	11208
Kristi Albers	66	71	69	206	9510
Carolyn Hill	72	69	66	207	8041
Alice Ritzman	70	69	68	207	8041
Jane Crafter	70	69	68	207	8041

September 11-13
PING-CELLULAR ONE CHAMPIONSHIP
COLUMBIA EDGEWATER COUNTRY CLUB
PORTLAND, OR

* Nancy Lopez	70	70	69	209	$67500
Jane Crafter	64	73	72	209	41891
Jan Stephenson	72	72	66	210	27172
Tina Barrett	66	69	75	210	27172
Donna Andrews	72	71	68	211	16152
Caroline Keggi	70	71	70	211	16152
Marta Figueras-Dotti	68	72	71	211	16152
Michelle McGann	72	72	69	213	11208
Judy Dickinson	71	70	72	213	11208
Helen Alfredsson	74	72	68	214	7849
Carolyn Hill	71	74	69	214	7849
Janice Gibson	69	74	71	214	7849
Rosie Jones	70	72	72	214	7849
Martha Faulconer	71	70	73	214	7849
Meg Mallon	69	72	73	214	7849

There were back-to-back wins for Nancy Lopez in September

September 17-20
SAFECO CLASSIC
MERIDIAN VALLEY COUNTRY CLUB, KENT, WA

Colleen Walker	72	67	68	70	277	$67500
Vicki Fergon	72	70	68	69	279	36230
Rosie Jones	71	69	70	69	279	36230
Debbie Massey	71	69	73	67	280	23776
Hollis Stacy	78	62	73	68	281	14174
Nancy Ramsbottom	73	70	68	70	281	14174

Dottie Mochrie	69	72	68	72	281	14174
Patty Sheehan	71	69	69	72	281	14174
Helen Alfredsson	71	68	70	72	281	14174
Kim Williams	71	71	72	68	282	9057
Nancy Lopez	71	71	71	69	282	9057
Juli Inkster	73	67	71	72	283	7925

September 24-27

LOS COYOTES LPGA CLASSIC

LOS COYOTES COUNTRY CLUB, BUENA PARK, CA

Nancy Scranton	73	68	73	65	279	$75000
Meg Mallon	68	73	69	70	280	46546
Susie Redman	73	71	69	68	281	33966
Kathy Postlewait	72	72	67	71	282	23902
Jan Stephenson	71	69	67	75	282	23902
Janice Gibson	70	72	72	69	283	16228

Dottie Mochrie won tour individual titles in 1992; she also teamed up with Dan Forsman to win the JC Penney Classic

Sherri Steinhauer	71	70	73	69	283	16228
Dale Eggeling	75	69	72	68	284	12454
Donna Andrews	71	70	68	75	284	12454
Nancy Lopez	72	74	70	69	285	10077
Betsy King	68	70	72	75	285	10077

November 6-8

MAZDA JAPAN CLASSIC

MUSASHIGAOKA GOLF CLUB, HANNO CITY,
SAITAMA-KEN, JAPAN

* Betsy King	66	72	67	205	$97500
Helen Alfredsson	68	66	71	205	60510
Alice Ritzman	67	69	70	206	44156
Anne Marie Palli	70	73	66	209	34344
Tina Barrett	73	71	66	210	20474
Nayoko Yoshikawa	72	68	70	210	20474
Donna Andrews	69	71	70	210	20474
Laura Davies	68	72	70	210	20474
Nancy Scranton	71	67	72	210	20474
Deb Richard	70	69	72	211	12552
Michelle McGann	69	70	72	211	12552
Barb Mucha	66	72	73	211	12552

December 3-6

J C PENNEY CLASSIC

INNISBROOK RESORT, TARPON SPRINGS, FL

Dottie Mochrie/Dan Forsman						
	66	63	66	69	264	$110000
Beth Daniel/Davis Love III						
	67	65	65	71	268	68000
Pat Bradley/Bill Glasson						
	67	69	70	64	270	31887
Brandie Burton/Billy Mayfair						
	68	67	68	67	270	31887
Debbie Massey/Mark McCumber						
	67	66	70	67	270	31887
Amy Benz/John Huston						
	67	69	65	69	270	31887
Tracy Kerdyk/Bruce Fleisher						
	68	69	69	65	271	17500
Sally Little/Fulton Allem						
	69	68	67	67	271	17500
Colleen Walker/Lee Janzen						
	71	70	67	64	272	12000
Amy Alcott/Duffy Waldorf						
	67	68	66	71	272	12000

1992 · LPGA WINNERS SUMMARY

OLDSMOBILE LPGA CLASSIC	C. Walker	SHOPRITE LPGA CLASSIC	A. M. Palli
PHAR-MOR AT INVERRARY	S. Hamlin	LADY KEYSTONE OPEN	D. Ammaccapane
ITOKI HAWAIIAN OPEN	L. Walters	ROCHESTER INTERNATIONAL	P. Sheehan
KEMPER OPEN	D. Coe	JAMIE FARR TOLEDO CLASSIC	P. Sheehan
INAMORI CLASSIC	J. Dickinson	THE PHAR-MOR IN YOUNGSTOWN	B. King
PING/WELCH'S CHAMPIONSHIP	B. Burton	JAL BIG APPLE CLASSIC	J. Inkster
STANDARD REGISTER PING	D. Ammaccapane	U.S. WOMEN'S OPEN CHAMPIONSHIP	P. Sheehan
NABISCO DINAH SHORE	D. Mochrie	WELCH'S CLASSIC	D. Mochrie
LAS VEGAS INTERNATIONAL	D. Lofland	MCCALL'S AT STRATTON MOUNTAIN	F. Descampe
SEGA CHAMPIONSHIP	D. Mochrie	DU MAURIER LTD CLASSIC	S. Steinhauer
SARA LEE CLASSIC	M. Will	NORTHGATE COMPUTER CLASSIC	K. Tschetter
CENTEL CLASSIC	D. Ammaccapane	SUN-TIMES CHALLENGE	D. Mochrie
CRESTAR-FARM FRESH CLASSIC	J. Wyatt	RAIL CHARITY GOLF CLASSIC	N. Lopez
MAZDA LPGA CHAMPIONSHIP	B. King	PING-CELLULAR ONE CHAMPIONSHIP	N. Lopez
LPGA CORNING CLASSIC	C. Walker	SAFECO CLASSIC	C. Walker
MCDONALD'S CHAMPIONSHIP	A. Okamoto	LOS COYOTES LPGA CLASSIC	N. Scranton
OLDSMOBILE CLASSIC	B. Mucha	MAZDA JAPAN CLASSIC	B. King

Third in the US Open, Donna Andrews is one of the leading young players on the LPGA Tour

Ping   Women's   Golf   Year

1992 · LPGA TOUR MONEY LIST: TOP 50

1	Dottie Mochrie	$693,335	18	Michelle McGann	239,062	34	Shelley Hamlin	157,327
2	Betsy King	551,320	19	Pat Bradley	238,541	35	Jane Crafter	155,485
3	Danielle Ammaccapane	513,639	20	Ayako Okamoto	229,953	36	Cindy Rarick	155,303
4	Brandie Burton	419,571	21	Liselotte Neumann	225,667	37	Tammie Green	154,717
5	Patty Sheehan	418,622	22	Missie Berteotti	213,720	38	Anne Marie Palli	153,065
6	Meg Mallon	400,052	23	Nancy Scranton	213,225	39	Laura Davies	150,163
7	Juli Inkster	392,063	24	Florence Descampe	210,281	40	Amy Benz	141,673
8	Nancy Lopez	382,128	25	Rosie Jones	204,096	41	Dale Eggeling	138,781
9	Colleen Walker	368,600	26	Alice Ritzman	201,922	42	Jan Stephenson	132,634
10	Judy Dickinson	351,559	27	Barb Mucha	190,519	43	Michelle Estill	132,399
11	Beth Daniel	329,681	28	Tina Barrett	184,719	44	Hollis Stacy	132,323
12	Sherri Steinhauer	315,145	29	JoAnne Carner	175,880	45	Marta Figueras-Dotti	127,789
13	Donna Andrews	299,839	30	Kristi Albers	173,189	46	Maggie Will	126,428
14	Dana Lofland	270,413	31	Caroline Keggi	172,669	47	Mitzi Edge	117,835
15	Deb Richard	266,427	32	Jane Geddes	164,127	48	Pamela Wright	116,775
16	Helen Alfredsson	262,115	33	Kris Tschetter	157,436	49	Karen Noble	110,278
17	Dawn Coe	251,392				50	Elaine Crosby	109,125

1992 · LPGA TOUR STATISTICS

ROLEX PLAYER OF THE YEAR

RK	NAME	POINTS
1	Dottie Mochrie	54
2	Betsy King	38
3	Danielle Ammaccapane	34
T4	Nancy Lopez	32
T4	Patty Sheehan	32
6	Colleen Walker	31
7	Brandie Burton	29
8	Beth Daniel	28
9	Judy Dickinson	25
10	Juli Inkster	22

VARE TROPHY

RK	NAME	AVG	RDS
1	Dottie Mochrie	70.80	91
2	Meg Mallon	70.99	84
3	Nancy Lopez	71.05	73
4	Patty Sheehan	71.30	77
5	Brandie Burton	71.30	83
6	Juli Inkster	71.43	84
7	Ayako Okamoto	71.48	52
8	Betsy King	71.50	96
9	Pat Bradley	71.60	87
10	Danielle Ammaccapane	71.60	93

GATORADE ROOKIE OF THE YEAR

RK	NAME	POINTS
1	Helen Alfredsson	867
2	Florence Descampe	723
3	Kelly Robbins	536
4	Angie Ridgeway	434
5	Karen Noble	352
6	Denise Baldwin	282
7	Michele Redman	252
8	Julie Larsen	234
9	Kate Golden	162
10	Kim Saiki	128

TOP 10 FINISHES:
D Mochrie

DRIVING DISTANCE:
M McGann

DRIVING ACCURACY:
N Ramsbottom

GREENS IN REGULATION:
N Lopez

PUTTING:
A Okamoto

SAND SAVES:
B Burton

BIRDIES:
M McGann

EAGLES:
M McGann

ROUNDS IN 60S:
D Mochrie

Dottie Mochrie

AMERICAN GOLFER OF THE YEAR

A Profile by Sonja Steptoe

Golf historians following the women's game will record 1992 as the year of Mochrie's moxie. Every so often, the ladies' tour needs an attitude adjuster - a dynamic personality who stirs things up, turns heads and reminds the rest of the world that women's golf is serious business too. Seven years ago, it was Pat Bradley, sending chills through galleries with her icy intensity while winning three of the four major championships. Never mind what the etiquette books said, Bradley made staring cool.

This time around, the rabble-rouser is 1992 LPGA Player of the Year Dottie Pepper Mochrie. Her four victories, including her first Major - the Nabisco Dinah Shore, along with the $693,000 in prize money she pocketed last season, catapulted her to the top of the sport at the tender age of 27. In just five seasons on tour, she has amassed six titles and $1.7 million in earnings.

At a glance, Mochrie would seem to be a Bradley clone who simply copied her hero's frosty stares and take-no-prisoners persona. But this blond-haired, blue-eyed dynamo is an original. Beneath those glacial glares of hers lies a blazing spirit. No one but Mochrie punctuates each triumph with a clinch-fisted cheer, and every setback with a fiery scowl. She is women golf's raging soul sister. Its blast furnace. And as she conquers, she captivates. 'Dottie's got such determination and such fire,' says fellow LPGA member Jane Geddes, a self-described Mochrie fan. 'I love watching her play.'

Her college coach, Furman University's Mic Potter, observes: 'She's got a drive most people can't even begin to understand.' Much of that drive is hereditary. Mochrie's father, Don Pepper, did a brief stint with baseball's Detroit Tigers in the big leagues in 1966. Pepper didn't take losses or hitting slumps well. 'One night he hit the wall of the dugout so hard, I thought he broke his hand,' recalls Lynn Pepper, Mochrie's mother. 'Some people don't show their emotions. But that's not our makeup.'

Some of Mochrie's drive is self-generated. 'She was definitely a type-A kid,' her mother says. No matter what little Dottie tackled, she managed to wrestle it to the ground. 'Whatever the standard was, I compared myself to it and tried to be better,' she says.

She was a whiz on the ski slopes, and so quick at study on the ivories that her piano teacher begged her to become a music major in college. But by that time, Dorothy Pepper had bought her grammar-school aged granddaughter a junior set of Chi Chi Rodriguez golf clubs and imbued her with a love for the game. Eventually, Don Pepper bought a driving range near the family home in Saratoga Springs, N.Y., and little Dottie became his best customer and prized pupil.

Against such fierce competition, the piano didn't stand a chance.

Mochrie's playing partners at her hometown MacGregor Links Golf Club were the first to witness the feistiness that would become her trademark. Minutes after 11-year-old Dottie lost 10 and 8 to a 16-year-old boy in the first round of a junior tournament, a group of boys eagerly asked if she was ready to hang up her spikes. 'No way,' she snapped, as she hoisted her bag of clubs over her shoulder and headed to the practice tee. A year later, she made it to the semi-finals of the tournament.

By the time she was in the ninth grade at Saratoga Springs High, she was the top player on the varsity squad, having petitioned the state Board of Education for permission to play with the boys as an eight grader because she was good and because there was no girls' squad.

In those days, her intense will to win made her a fearsome match-play competitor and earned her three New York State Junior and Amateur titles, as well as membership on the 1981 Junior World Cup Team. In college, though, she had to contain that aggressiveness and learn to compete in the more conservative stroke-play format. Not an easy adjustment for the young woman affectionately nicknamed 'Hot Pepper.' Time and again during her freshman year, coach Potter reminded her to play the golf course, instead of her opponents. And time and again, Mochrie's competitive urges got the best of her.

The transformation began at the end of her second year at Furman, during the final round of the women's collegiate championship. She was in the last group, paired with her two arch rivals, Deb Richard of Univ. of Florida, and Jody Rosenthal (now Anschutz), of Univ. of Tulsa. The individual title was up for grabs and the three women went after each other with a vengeance. None of them broke 75. Mochrie wound up losing the individual title by a stroke to upstart Danielle Ammaccapane of Arizona State. 'We all got sucked into believing it was between us and Danielle snuck in,' Mochrie recalls wistfully.

Since then, Mochrie has played by Potter's rule: get it in the hole somehow; and get it there fast. Though she never won that national collegiate title, she collected her share of amateur laurels. She was a three-time All-American and the low amateur at the 1984 US Womens' Open. Her performance at the Open impressed Judy Bell, who captained the US Curtis Cup team Mochrie played on later the same year. 'Dottie's strong in every department,' Bell says. 'She's a great ball striker and such a good iron player. But if she misses a green, she's got the shots to get it up close.'

Somewhere along the way, however, Mochrie's tenacity became more curse than blessing. After winning her LPGA playing card on the first try in 1987, she hit the tour like a house afire, winning tournaments and becoming the fastest millionaire in LPGA history. In her wake, however, was a scorched path, lined with peers who'd been burned by her aloof, cocky attitude. 'She was the first young player to come along in 15 years whose only goal when she got a four-shot lead was to increase it to 10,' an LPGA official told *Golf World* magazine. 'She didn't want to beat the other players. She wanted to insult them.'

Adding injury to insult, Mochrie sometimes trampled the rules of golf etiquette on the way to her next shot in her early days on tour. She hurled clubs and shouted orders at her airborne golf balls. 'We all yell at the ball,' quipped an LPGA veteran after watching Mochrie's antics during a round. 'But Dottie's the only one who expects it to listen.'

It wasn't that Mochrie didn't have a sense of humour. All it takes is one look at her earlobes - eight holes in total, each occupied by a diamond stud or a gold hoop - to see that she has a whimsical side. But how to turn down the flame on her burning ambition? 'I looked around a few years ago,' she told *Golf World,* 'and I wasn't happy with the person I'd become.'

'She tries so hard,' says Doug Mochrie, her husband of seven years. 'She's like a walking time bomb.'

For a while, she also was like a walking hospital ward. The file on Mochrie's stress-related maladies in recent years includes colitis, ulcers and a hiatal hernia. About four years ago, her doctors ordered her to calm down. To make sure she obeyed, Doug quit his job as club pro at the Saratoga Golf & Polo Club in 1990 to join her on tour. Her colleagues noticed the difference immediately. 'When she had other caddies, she was wild,' Jane Geddes remembers. 'Doug has calmed her down. They're a team, the Mochries.'

It certainly looks that way. Doug, a tall blond who wears a jewelled stud in his left earlobe, drives his wife to the clubhouse everyday, totes her clubs, helps her line up her tee shots, and then after a round, stands on the driving range with her, correcting any minor swing flaws. They travel with their dog, Shank, a cinnamon chowchow that Dottie now dotes on as much as her scorecard. Life, according to Mrs Mochrie, 'is just one big party! I'm learning to take the bad days better. Golf isn't a matter of life and death anymore.'

Her flame may have dimmed. But make no mistake: Mochrie's fire still burns. She proved that last season, in several memorable final-round performances. She shot a 69 on the last day of the Dinah Shore to force a playoff with a dazed Juli Inkster, who bogied the 18th hole before losing the title on the first extra hole. After sealing the win, Mochrie leaped into her husband's outstretched arms and burst into tears. Then, at the Sega Women's Championship in Atlanta, Georgia, a week after Fred Couples' stirring victory at nearby Augusta National, Mochrie brilliantly played bump-and-run with a 35 foot, downhill chip shot from the back of the 18th green. When the ball stopped eight inches from the cup and she tapped in for birdie and the victory, the crowd erupted and several good old boys even shouted: 'You're the Woman!'

But perhaps the most memorable or most poignant accomplishment of Mochrie's season came at the end, during the Wendy's Three Tour Challenge. She was part of the LPGA contingent, along with Nancy Lopez and Patty Sheehan, that battled teams from the PGA and the Senior PGA Tours. Her Senior opponent on the last day was Jack Nicklaus, who along with Bradley is one of Mochrie's childhood idols. When she and Nicklaus reached the 18th hole, he had a 15-footer for birdie that would have forced a playoff. Mochrie had an 8-footer to save par and ensure victory for the LPGA side. Nicklaus missed; Mochrie didn't.

That single stroke of her putter did much to elevate the status of women's golf: it made the gentlemen sit up and take notice of the ladies. Said a clearly impressed Nicklaus: 'Dottie's terrific. She has a lot of talent and a lot of moxie.'

And at that momentous instant, Mochrie became rubber and the LPGA became glue. The praise from Nicklaus bounced off her and stuck to the tour. She had done more than simply win a made-for-TV team match. She had given it clinch-fisted, fiery-eyed moxie. Mochrie's moxie.

Husband and caddie, Doug with Dottie at the British Open

Sonja Steptoe is a Sports Illustrated staff writer.

P i n g   W o m e n ' s   G o l f   Y e a r

Amateur Golf in America

As the Americans bathed, the Europeans threatened to run off with all of their clothes. In 1992 America's amateur women surrendered the Curtis Cup and the Espirito Trophy (Vancouver's World Amateur Team Championship), both following the Solheim Cup across the Atlantic. Modesty was only salvaged by Vicki Goetze, the 19-year-old phenomenon from Georgia who claimed both the US Women's Amateur and NCAA Championships at the expense of the brilliant Swedish player, Annika Sorenstam.

Goetze's second US Amateur triumph is reviewed overleaf; to win two national titles before the age of 20 is an extraordinary achievement, but her first success in the NCAA was where she in fact produced her most impressive golf of the year.

After three day's play over the testing Karsten GC course in Phoenix, the four round stroke-play championship had developed into an absorbing matchplay-style contest between the two leading college stars, Goetze, and the defending champion, Sorenstam. The Swede looked in a strong position to retain her title, being three ahead of her rival after compiling rounds of 72-68-72. She then produced a very solid closing 71 but was eclipsed when Goetze stormed to victory with a fantastic final day 65. That round was a course record and her 280 total was a championship record; three back on 283, Sorenstam finished six strokes ahead of the third placed player and nine ahead of the player who finished fourth.

The American amateur scene is due to lose both Goetze and Sorenstam next year as each attempts to plunder, respectively, the professional tours in America and Europe.

Goetze's Curtis Cup partner, Amy Fruhwirth, winner of the 1992 USGA Public Links Championship, has similar aspirations for 1993. Who then will fill the void? The stock answer for the last 20 years or so has been Carol Semple Thompson plus one or two talented youngsters. Last year Semple Thompson was 43 when she won her third consecutive Harder Hall tournament in Florida and competed in her seventh Curtis Cup, and 44 when she reached the semi-finals of the US Amateur.

As for the talented youngsters, Californians Emilee Klein and Kellee Booth would appear to be the two names to watch out for - at least that is, one presumes, until the lure of the twenty million dollar plus LPGA Tour becomes just too strong to resist.

In 1992 Vicki Goetze was once again America's outstanding women's amateur player

US Women's Amateur Championship

To win the US Women's Amateur crown is to walk into the legendary shadow cast by the great Glenna Collett Vare, in much the same way as the men who win their Amateur Championship bask in the reflected glory of Bobby Jones - Mrs Vare won six Women's Amateur titles, Mr Jones won five men's.

Many of the great names of women's golf have followed Glenna Collett Vare, notably Patty Berg, Babe Zaharias, JoAnne Carner and, in more recent times, Beth Daniel and Juli Inkster. Only time will tell if 1992's champion deserves to be mentioned in such company; one can comment, however, that the first 19 years of Vicki Goetze's life suggest that there is every possibility.

Goetze, a native of Wisconsin, but raised in Georgia, has now won two US Amateurs, the first being in 1989 when she was just 16. She beat Brandie Burton in that '89 final and Burton is now a major force on the LPGA Tour. Great things are also being predicted for Annika Sorenstam, the Swedish player whom Goetze defeated in the 1992 final at Kemper Lakes.

Sorenstam had breezed into the 36 hole final beating Abby Pearson 7 and 5 in the quarter-final and Pat Cornett-Iker by 7 and 6 in the semi-final. Many people predicted that the 6345 yards, par 72 layout would favour the longer-hitting Swede.

Goetze herself was in tremendous form. To reach the final she won all her five matches by comprehensive margins. It turned out to be a good, if not a great final: one that Goetze appeared to have taken control of when she made three birdies early in the afternoon round. With six holes to play, she seemed to be coasting until her lapses combined with a superb stroke from Sorenstam at the 35th saw them all square walking to the final tee. Earlier in the summer, in a similar situation at Hoylake in the Curtis Cup, Goetze had failed to rise to the occasion; but this time it was her opponent who folded under the pressure, hitting her approach into water. Goetze found the green and duly won her second US Women's Amateur title. 'She's still not long enough off the tee' is the remark frequently directed at the champion. Sure. Try telling that to Annika Sorenstam.

August 10 - 15
1992 US WOMEN'S AMATEUR CHAMPIONSHIP
KEMPER LAKES, ILLINOIS

QUARTER-FINALS:
V Goetze beat T Hanson 4 and 3
A Sorenstam (Sweden) beat M A Pearson 7 and 5
C Semple Thompson beat A Fruhwirth 1 hole
P Cornett-Iker beat E Port 2 holes

SEMI-FINALS:
V Goetze beat C Semple Thompson 5 and 4
A Sorenstam beat P Cornett-Iker 7 and 6

FINAL
V GOETZE beat A SORENSTAM 1 hole

· ROLL OF HONOUR ·

1895	Mrs C S Brown	1935	Glenna Collett Vare	1978	Cathy Sherk
1896	Beatrix Hoyt	1936	Pam Barton (GB)	1979	Carolyn Hill
1897	Beatrix Hoyt	1937	Mrs Julius Page	1980	Juli Inkster
1898	Beatrix Hoyt	1938	Patty Berg	1981	Juli Inkster
1899	Ruth Underhill	1939	Betty Jameson	1982	Juli Inkster
1900	Frances Griscom	1940	Betty Jameson	1983	Joanne Pacillo
1901	Genevieve Hecker	1941	Elizabeth Hicks Newell	1984	Deb Richard
1902	Genevieve Hecker	1942-5	No competition	1985	Michiko Hattori (Jap)
1903	Bessie Anthony	1946	Babe Zaharias	1986	Kay Cockerill
1904	Georgianna Bishop	1947	Louise Suggs	1987	Kay Cockerill
1905	Pauline Mackay	1948	Grace Lenczyk	1988	Pearl Sinn
1906	Harriot Curtis	1949	Dorothy Germain Porter	1989	Vicki Goetze
1907	Margaret Curtis	1950	Beverly Hanson	1990	Patty Hurst
1908	Kate Harley	1951	Dorothy Kirby	1991	Amy Fruhwirth
1909	Dorothy Campbell (GB)	1952	Jacqueline Pung	1992	Vicki Goetze
1910	Dorothy Campbell (GB)	1953	Mary Lena Faulk		
1911	Margaret Curtis	1954	Barbara Romack		
1912	Margaret Curtis	1955	Patricia Lesser		
1913	Gladys Ravenscroft (GB)	1956	Marlene Stewart (Can)		
1914	Kate Harley Jackson	1957	JoAnne Gunderson		
1915	Mrs C H Vanderbeck	1958	Anne Quast		
1916	Alexa Stirling	1959	Barbara McIntire		
1917	No competition	1960	JoAnne Gunderson		
1918	No competition	1961	Anne Quast Decker		
1919	Alexa Stirling	1962	JoAnne Gunderson		
1920	Alexa Stirling	1963	Anne Quast Welts		
1921	Marion Hollins	1964	Barbara McIntire		
1922	Glenna Collett	1965	Jean Ashley		
1923	Edith Cummings	1966	JoAnne Gunderson Carner		
1924	Dorothy Campbell Hurd (GB)	1967	Mary Lou Dill		
1925	Glenna Collett	1968	JoAnne Gunderson Carner		
1926	Helen Stetson	1969	Catherine Lacoste (Fr)		
1927	Miriam Burns Horn	1970	Martha Wilkinson		
1928	Glenna Collett	1971	Laura Baugh		
1929	Glenna Collett	1972	Mary Anee Budke		
1930	Glenna Collett	1973	Carol Semple		
1931	Helen Hicks	1974	Cynthia Hill		
1932	Virginia Van Wie	1975	Beth Daniel		
1933	Virginia Van Wie	1976	Donna Horton		
1934	Virginia Van Wie	1977	Beth Daniel		

Vicki Goetze

5 Europe

1992 WPG European Tour Review

How do you review the 1992 women's professional season in Europe without mentioning the Solheim Cup - already detailed in this book - when all that Europe's women golfers seem to want to talk about is the Solheim Cup? It is a bit like being invited to write a chapter on great golfing personalities without referring to Lee Trevino and Nancy Lopez.

There is, of course, no escaping the fact that the momentous result at Dalmahoy in October is potentially the most significant single happening in the history of European women's golf. The key word though must be 'potentially', as for one thing it is too early to judge. If confidence has a great influence on performance then it does seem likely that Europe's top players will go from strength to strength, climb the world rankings ladder and win more frequently. But what percentage of those feats will be performed in Europe is another matter. It is no secret that the WPGE Tour would like to host more events and that several of its 'leading lights' plan to play much of their golf in America in 1993; yet there is surely a lot more cause for optimism than pessimism.

The Tour's 1993 calendar of events is being shaped and reshaped as I write, but regarding those 'leading lights' playing in America (a number of European players won LPGA Tour cards late last year) two things are worth emphasising. Firstly, golf in Europe has never suffered from Europeans playing and winning in America - quite the opposite in fact, besides, those who play poorly overseas soon come home! Secondly, the majority of the travelling stars still intend to compete frequently in Europe, this being for a combination of factors including loyalty, 'roots' and the simple reason that most greatly enjoy playing in Europe.

There is a genuinely international and, without wanting to sound pompous, multicultural flavour to professional golf in the 'Old World'. In terms of venue this was less evident in 1992 because of the limited schedule, but there were still tournaments in Britain, France, Belgium, Spain, Germany, Holland, Sweden, Italy and even, for the first time, Slovenia, with post season events being staged in Dubai and Taiwan. (The first WPGE Tour event of 1993 was held in, of all places, Malaysia). As for the players themselves, at the last count 27 nationalities were represented on the tour.

How then, three rainy days in Scotland aside, will 1992 be remembered in Europe? The record books will suggest that this was a season dominated by England's Laura Davies and Sweden's Helen Alfredsson. Between them they won five of the twelve events (and neither entered the first two or the last). Davies won three times: the European Open in Germany by two shots; the Italian Open by five and the English

Open by seven. Of the nine events she entered she finished outside of the top ten just once. Alfredsson brilliantly captured the prestigious Hennessy Cup in Cologne and later the IBM Open in front of an enthusiastic home crowd in Stockholm; she played in only five tournaments and her

Saunders Award, see page 112) best illustrate how far in front of their European rivals the 'Big Two' were in 1992. A final pair of statistics also merits a mention: Davies was 75 under par for the 34 rounds she played in Europe and Alfredsson was 50 under par for 19 rounds. Little wonder then

A year that began, at best, indifferently ended magnificently for Europe's Number One, Laura Davies

worst finish was sixth (this in a year when she was named Rookie of the Year in America and won in Japan!) In both the official Money List and stroke averages, Davies came first and Alfredsson second. Perhaps the stroke averages (for the Vivien

that whenever they competed they tended to dominate.

In addition to Davies' hatrick of wins, there were three other English successes and they happened in successive tournaments. Following early season triumphs in Australia and South East Asia, Alison Nicholas visited Versailles and won the AGF Open de Paris; in the next event Kitrina Douglas and Trish Johnson turned the BMW European Masters into the 'Bristol Masters' - the two westcountry players having pulled away from a very strong field battled head-to-head on the final day with Douglas eventually emerging the winner, but then it became Johnson's turn to collect first prize at the Skol La Manga Classic, thanks chiefly to a 27-putt third round 66.

Bristolians in Brussels: Kitrina Douglas (left) and Trish Johnson at the BMW European Masters

Although British players won the most tournaments in 1992 (Scotland's perennial champion, Dale Reid, won the Emirates Challenge in Dubai to add to the tally above) Swedish golfers made at least as big an impact. The Laura Davies-Alison Nicholas partnership was the most talked about in the Solheim Cup but the Helen Alfredsson and Lotte Neumann pairing was also undefeated and, along with Catrin Nilsmark who of course holed the winning putt, three of Europe's final day seven points came from the all-conquering Swedish trio. Two weeks after the Solheim Cup Alfredsson and Neumann teamed up again to win the Sunrise World Team Championship in typhoon-hit Taiwan

P i n g   W o m e n ' s   G o l f   Y e a r

(the tournament is reviewed on pages 128-130) - in second place was the English team of Laura Davies and Trish Johnson.

Both Neumann and Alfredsson played a fairly limited amount in Europe last year but Nilsmark competed and seemed to feature prominently in almost every event. Twice the striking 24-year-old finished runner-up and with her confidence sky-high after her celebrated exploits at Dalmahoy not many doubt that she will win soon. Also waiting in the wings, and seemingly destined to claim a prominent position on centre stage, are Carin Hjalmarsson and Annika Sorenstam. 1992 was Hjalmarsson's rookie season on tour and she demonstrated her exceptional gifts by producing what is

widely regarded as the round of the year in Europe, a course record-shattering 64 in the third round of the English Open. As this event was staged at Tytherington, where the Tour's head-

A study in concentration: Catrin Nilsmark is one of Sweden's brightest young stars – and there are many

quarters are based, she certainly picked her moment to play the best round of her life. Sorenstam, meanwhile, has been making a big name for herself overseas. In 1991 she was the college champion of America and last year she finished runner-up in the US Amateur Championship to Vicki Goetze. Sorenstam gained revenge over the US Curtis Cup star late in the year, when she convincingly claimed the leading individual prize at the World Amateur Team Championship in Vancouver (see page 131). Needless to say her professional debut in Europe is eagerly awaited - and feared!

Sweden does not of course have a monopoly of emerging talent: Great Britain and Ireland won the Curtis Cup in 1992 - since which time the 18-year-old heroine of the final day, Caroline Hall, has turned professional, while Spain's amateur team won the aforementioned World Amateur Team Championship defeating Sorenstam's Sweden (and, for that matter, Vicki Goetze's America). Spain already has

At just 19 years of age, Sandrine Mendiburu became Europe's Rookie of the Year

two players knocking on the Solheim Cup selection door, namely Xonia Wunsch-Ruiz and Tania Abitbol. And then there are the French...

It is one of the great mysteries of men's golf that despite a great surge in interest over the past decade or so, not to mention the proliferation of excellent golf courses, no major stars have surfaced in recent times from France. The same however cannot be said of the ladies' game; in the late eighties the elegant Marie Laure de Lorenzi rivalled Laura Davies as the leading golfer in Europe and last season it was two outstanding young French players who duelled with Sweden's Carin Hjalmarsson for the Rookie of the

Ping Women's Golf Year

Year prize.

After winning the French, Italian and British amateur titles in 1991, Valerie Michaud must have wondered what else there was to win in the amateur game; she thus turned professional and played in only eight tournaments before claiming a first

a teenager until last December time isn't exactly against her!

Nor is it against the charismatic and effervescent 21-year-old Italian Stefania Croce, whose joie de vivre charmed the huge Woburn crowds during the opening event of the 1992 season and whose splendid

(Below) Spain's Xonia Wunsch-Ruiz, and (right) Alison Nicholas

WPGE Tour title - the Holiday Inn Leiden Open in Holland. Arguably even more impressive were the consistently strong performances of Sandrine Mendiburu from Bayonne. A series of high finishes enabled the former US Girls champion to finish 10th on the European Money List and pip Hjalmarsson and Michaud for the Rookie of the Year prize. The only reason that she didn't win in 1992 was because Laura Davies played, 'So well it is ridiculous' in the Italian Open. Given that Mendiburu was

golf won her the same Ford Classic. Several of the famed 'leading lights' didn't compete at Woburn that week but the tournament didn't appear to suffer for it; more importantly, if there is truth in the suggestion that Croce might not have won if the likes of Neumann and Alfredsson had competed then Europe would have been denied seeing the coming of age of an exciting new star. Indeed, there is a great golfing paradox here: it maybe because it is easier to win in Europe than on the LPGA

Valerie Michaud, winner of the Holiday Inn Leiden Open. (Opposite page) The world's her oyster: at 23, Florence Descampe has already won in Europe and America

Tour that Europe's golfers have started to catch up - and in terms of the quality of very young talent perhaps even overhaul - their American counterparts. Would 23-year-old Belgian Florence Descampe have gained the confidence to win in her rookie year in America if she hadn't experienced winning repeatedly in Europe? Possibly not, but then Europe's star performers had better not grow too confident lest somebody like Patty Sheehan sails across the Atlantic and fires a warning shot across their bows - as she did at Woburn in the British Open!

And nor should the brilliant youngsters assume that they are about to stage a takeover in Europe. Past Order of Merit winners, Corrinne Dibnah and Marie Laure de Lorenzi came second and third respectively behind Sheehan at Woburn in October; moreover, just who on earth is going to tell Laura Davies that it is time to move over. Any offers?

Ping Women's Golf Year

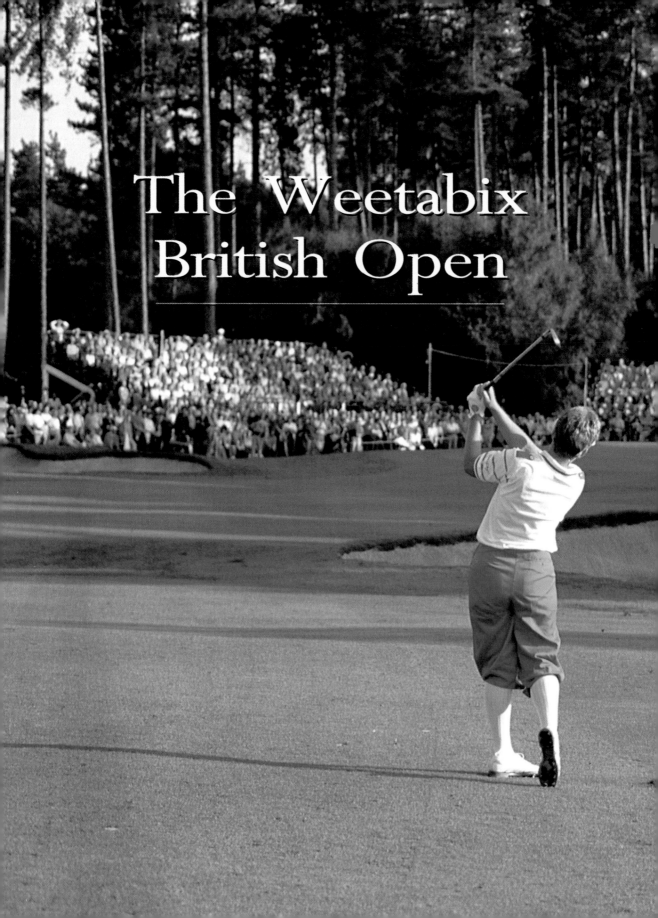

The Weetabix
British Open

The Weetabix British Open

By David MacLaren

As little as two weeks before the 1992 Weetabix Women's British Open at Woburn, anybody enquiring as to the chances of the reigning US Open Champion completing a transatlantic double would have been quoted odds even longer than those on offer for a European victory in the following week's Solheim Cup.

However proficient a player Sheehan is, and there may be none better, the week before the tournament even Patty herself viewed the possibility of a double triumph as something that even Nick Faldo (were he eligible!) wouldn't even dream about. The reason for such low expectations was due less to a lack of personal confidence as to an unhealthy dose of bureaucratic red tape which prevented most of the best players from America's LPGA Tour competing in one of ladies golf's bona-fide Majors.

Called in due to the late withdrawal of Marta Figueras Dotti, it is a tribute to the leading female exponent of Faldo-type dominance that Sheehan was able to paper over a lack of preparation - acclimatisation to British golf had come no less than twelve years previously during a Curtis Cup encounter - and sweep aside the assembled might of Europe's best lady golfers with a controlled display of precision golf.

Much of the somewhat hysterical pre-tournament talk centred around the certainty of Laura Davies capping a fine season by strolling to a victory that would provide a prelude to an equally inevitable European triumph at Dalmahoy. Such talk was at best premature, of course, and the fact that one of Britain's finest female sporting ambassadors was unable to add the British crown to her

Laura Davies' form strangely deserted her at Woburn

runaway victory in the previous European event, the BWW Italian Open (her third title of the year), serves only to underline the strength in depth of ladies' golf, and of course the prowess of one Patty Sheehan.

The American certainly did not open up as if she was treating the tournament merely as a warm up for the heat of battle to come at Dalmahoy. If she was simply practising, on the other hand, and a first round 68 represented no more than a 'stroll in the park', then her competitors should take heed when she really concentrates her mind!

To view the week at Woburn as no more

Patty Sheehan is on her way to an historic US-British Open double

Gallic flair – Marie Laure de Lorenzi of France finished third

more than a prelude to the main business of the year - the Solheim Cup - is akin to suggesting that Nick Faldo will be trying his damndest to win this year's Open Championship simply to accumulate some Ryder Cup points. The truth is that the Weetabix Women's British Open represents the pinnacle of the ladies' game in Europe, and is cementing its place as one of the world's most coveted tournaments. It possesses virtually every ingredient required for a successful major championship - a loyal and enthusiastic sponsor, a wonderful venue, and the knowledgeable support of the golfing public.

It would be nice to add the support of the British weather to the above list, but then again it has been known to snow in the UK at the end of September, and so small mercies must be gratefully accepted. Sheehan would probably have triumphed even on a snow covered Duke's course, although her elegant attire of plus-twos would presumably have been modified. The point is, of course, that great champions can adapt to and triumph in whatever conditions they are confronted with - be it the lushness of Augusta or the windswept bleakness of an East coast links.

The emerald, tree-lined fairways of the Duke's course fall within such extremes, but nevertheless contributed to a memorable spectacle. The early talk of a Davies victory was soon shown to be as wide of the mark as her opening drive and by the end of her first hole in the tournament she was already three shots behind her playing partner Sheehan. This was a position that would not be reversed until the dramatic events of the following week.

America's first lady of golf began with an almost flawless 68, a score that gained Patty almost as much respect as her post-round interview in which she nimbly trod a diplomatic tight rope in justifying her participation at Woburn: 'This tour needs some help right now and maybe if we help out, we will also be helping ourselves in the long term'. Well said.

sports had a temporarily debilitating effect when play resumed on Saturday, and by the end of the second round she found herself trailing the gutsy Australian Corinne Dibnah by one stroke.

That play was possible at all on Saturday was a tribute to all concerned and a

Australian runner-up Corinne Dibnah tries the next best thing to a spirit level

But never mind the long term - Sheehan was determined to add to her list of titles as soon as decently possible. She even managed to complete her triumph in three days instead of the usual four, due to the unfortunate but not unexpected intervention of a Friday morning deluge which beat the combined efforts of an army of greenkeepers, to say nothing of the prayers of experienced rainmaker Alex Hay. Rather than spend the time indulging in some soggy British culture, Sheehan chose instead to watch a movie about baseball. The change of

tremendous relief to ever-enthusiastic sponsor Richard George of Weetabix, whose disappointment the previous day had been concealed by a refreshingly British dose of optimism, 'Better today than the weekend when BBC are giving us live coverage.'

Watched by a record crowd, and an even more welcome visitor in the shape of the sun, Dibnah and Sheehan played the first nine holes on Sunday as a duel, firing intermittent birdies in an attempt to forge a commanding lead. For the Australian, the attempt was a brave but vain one, as the

Sheehan salutes the crowd at the 72nd hole relentless American saw off her challenge with a hatrick of birdies at the 13th, 15th and 16th. Others tried too and failed: leading French player Marie Laure de Lorenzi hinted at a timely return to form before running out of steam, whilst a second American superstar, Dottie Mochrie, briefly threatened the destiny of Sheehan's crown, before a run of dropped shots derailed her challenge.

When it was all over, the enormity of Patty Sheehan's achievement slowly began to dawn on both her and the assembled spectators. To win the US Open and the British Open during the course of a lifetime would be achievement enough, even for today's golfing perfectionists. To win both in the same year would prove a fitting finale to the most illustrious career, and the long-term significance was clearly not lost on an emotional Sheehan: 'I am so excited. Speechless really. Ever since I was told that the US and British had never been won in the same year it put a fire in my belly. Now I've done it, I don't know what to say. I'm proud and thrilled.' And Weetabix and Woburn have a worthy champion.

P i n g   W o m e n ' s   G o l f   Y e a r

The kiss that put the seal on a magnificent summer

THE 1992 WEETABIX BRITISH OPEN
24 - 27 SEPTEMBER • WOBURN G & CC

Patty Sheehan	68	72	67	207	£50,000	Pamela Wright	73	76	69	218	4,560
Corinne Dibnah	70	69	71	210	32,000	Kristal Parker	72	74	72	218	4,560
Marie Laure de Lorenzi	71	71	70	212	21,000	Jane Geddes	78	69	72	219	4,300
Liselotte Neumann	69	74	70	213	16,000	Dale Reid	73	73	74	220	4,060
Patti Rizzo	72	70	72	214	11,600	Alicia Dibos	75	75	70	220	4,060
Helen Alfredsson	74	72	68	214	11,600	Valerie Michaud	71	76	73	220	4,060
Dottie Mochrie	74	68	73	215	9,000	Tania Abitbol	72	71	78	221	3,550
Janice Arnold	70	74	72	216	6,120	Federica Dassu	73	77	71	221	3,550
Suzanne Strudwick	75	72	69	216	6,120	Trish Johnson	73	73	75	221	3,550
Florence Descampe	71	73	72	216	6,120	Li Wen-Lin	74	70	77	221	3,550
Malin Burstrom	72	73	71	216	6,120	Carin Hjalmarsson	74	75	72	221	3,550
Evelyn Orley	70	75	71	216	6,120	Cindy Figg-Currier	71	77	73	221	3,550
Karen Davies	75	70	73	218	4,560	Kathryn Marshall	74	73	74	221	3,550

1992 WPG European Tour Results

30 April - May 1
FORD CLASSIC
WOBURN G & CC (DUCHESS' COURSE)
MILTON KEYNES, ENGLAND

Stefania Croce	68	73	72	73	286	£9750
Trish Johnson	72	71	73	73	289	5575
Evelyn Orley	73	72	75	69	298	5575
Corinne Dibnah	73	75	72	70	290	3510
Jane Hill	76	71	72	72	291	2515
Karen Lunn	71	76	73	71	291	2515
Karinne Espinasse	70	73	75	74	292	1787
Linzi Fletcher	73	77	71	71	292	1787
Gillian Stewart	75	70	73	76	294	1456
Alison Nicholas	71	74	80	70	295	1204
Kim Lasken	76	77	73	69	295	1204
Maria Bertilskold	72	74	77	72	295	1204

7-10 May
AGF OPEN DE PARIS
GOLF DE LA BOULIE PARIS, FRANCE

Alison Nicholas	66	68	73	68	275	£12000
Alicia Dibos	65	70	74	67	276	8120
Dale Reid	72	75	69	65	281	4028
Suzanne Strudwick	67	74	70	70	281	4028
Catrin Nilsmark	71	71	70	69	281	4028
Sandrine Mendiburu	68	71	72	70	281	4028
Kitrina Douglas	73	67	70	72	282	2400
Kristal Parker	68	71	74	71	284	2000
Federica Dassu	73	70	71	71	285	1696
Susan Moon	68	73	72	72	285	1696

21 - 24 May
BMW EUROPEAN MASTERS
GOLF DU BERCUIT, BRUSSELS, BELGIUM

Kitrina Douglas	69	68	72	70	279	£21000
Trish Johnson	70	70	70	70	280	14210
Helen Alfredsson	69	72	71	70	282	9800
Stefania Croce	70	72	71	70	283	7560

Alicia Dibos	67	75	70	73	285	5936
Alison Nicholas	74	68	74	71	287	4200
Kristal Parker	73	68	76	70	287	4200
Lisa Hackney	76	68	73	70	287	4200
Laura Davies	73	73	72	71	289	2837
Suzanne Strudwick	72	72	72	73	289	2837
Page Dunlap	72	69	73	75	289	2837
Corinne Soules	71	76	75	68	290	2408

28-31 May
SKOL LA MANGA CLUB CLASSIC
LA MANGA CLUB (NORTH COURSE)
CARTAGENA, SPAIN

Trish Johnson	73	66	67	68	274	£9000
Florence Descampe	71	66	68	70	275	5145
Catrin Nilsmark	70	67	67	71	275	5145
Laura Davies	71	70	64	72	277	3240
Catherine Panton-Lewis	73	72	63	72	278	2322
Suzanne Strudwick	71	71	68	68	278	2322
Alison Nicholas	70	71	68	70	279	1548
Allison Shapcott	72	71	71	65	279	1548
LaRee Sugg	72	72	67	68	279	1548
Jane Shearwood	70	68	70	72	280	1200

25-28 June
EUROPEAN OPEN
BEUERBERG GOLF CLUB, MUNICH, GERMANY

Laura Davies	72	70	71	72	285	£15000
Cartin Nilsmark	68	73	73	74	287	10150
Sandrine Mendiburu	75	72	75	68	290	7000
Alicia Dibos	72	76	73	70	291	4820
Helen Dobson	75	73	71	72	291	4820
Sofia Gronberg	73	71	74	74	292	3000
Jane Geddes	73	69	73	77	292	3000
Helen Alfredsson	73	73	73	73	292	3000
Xonia Wunsch-Ruiz	76	68	74	75	293	2120
Kristal Parker	69	71	77	76	293	2120
Lora Fairclough	73	77	71	73	294	1840

Italian Stefania Croce was a hugely popular 'start-to-finish' winner of the Ford Classic

Ping   Women's   Golf   Year

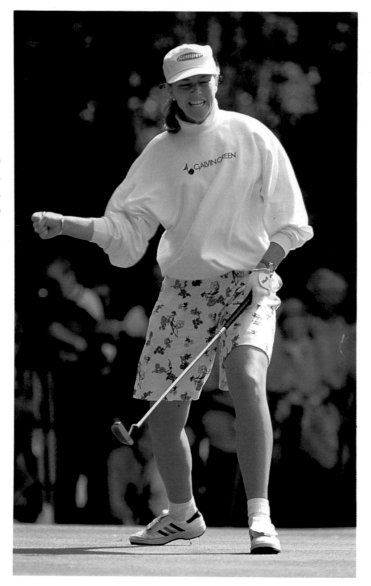

Helen Alfredsson won two of the five European events she entered in 1992

9-12 July

HENNESSY CUP

GOLF UND LANDCLUB KOLN, COLOGNE, GERMANY

Helen Alfredsson	68	70	67	66	271	£18000
Trish Johnson	67	66	67	72	272	12180
Laura Davies	66	66	73	68	273	7440
Liselotte Neumann	66	72	66	69	273	7440
Florence Descampe	70	69	66	71	276	5100
Alison Nicholas	72	66	70	70	278	4200
Lora Fairclough	69	70	70	70	279	3600
Marie Laure de Lorenzi	70	70	70	70	280	3600
Suzanne Strudwick	68	71	71	72	282	2550
Leigh Ann Mills	72	73	70	67	282	2550
Kitrina Douglas	70	73	72	69	284	2210
Karen Lunn	77	69	67	72	285	1915
Xonia Wunsch-Ruiz	71	73	72	69	285	1915
Catrin Nilsmark	72	74	69	70	285	1915
Helen Wadsworth	74	71	68	72	285	1915

30 July - 2 August
ENGLISH OPEN
THE TYTHERINGTON CLUB, CHESHIRE, ENGLAND

Laura Davies	72	69	69	71	281	£7500
Tania Abitbol	69	72	75	72	288	3348
Marie Laure de Lorenzi	71	71	75	72	288	3348
Corinne Dibnah	73	69	73	73	288	3348
Alison Nicholas	69	79	70	70	288	3348
Trish Johnson	74	72	75	68	289	1625
Catrin Nilsmark	72	72	74	71	289	1625
Suzanne Strudwick	74	72	73	71	290	1250
Elisabeth Aron-Quelhas	77	73	67	74	291	1120
Carin Hjalmarsson	75	64	73	80	292	1000
Dale Reid	70	70	77	68	293	920
Marjan De Boer	78	74	74	68	294	860

21-23 August
HOLIDAY INN LEIDEN OPEN
RIJSWIJK GOLF & BUSINESS CENTRE
NR ROTTERDAM, HOLLAND

Valerie Michaud	67	68	69	204	£8250
Laura Davies	69	69	67	205	5580
Gillian Stewart	69	72	68	209	3410
Catrin Nilsmark	72	68	69	209	3410
Lora Fairclough	71	66	75	212	2330
Federica Dassu	74	66	73	213	1545
Marie Laure de Lorenzi	69	68	76	213	1545
Dale Reid	71	71	71	213	1545
Tammie Green	71	69	73	213	1545
Corinne Dibnah	71	71	72	214	1056
Shani Waugh	70	70	74	214	1056

27-30 August
IBM OPEN
HANINGE GOLF CLUB, STOCKHOLM, SWEDEN

Helen Alfredsson	68	70	71	69	278	£13500
Liselotte Neumann	73	70	69	68	280	9135
Laura Davies	68	72	72	71	283	6300
Annika Sorenstam	69	70	72	72	283	Amateur
Janice Arnold	72	72	70	70	284	4860
Trish Johnson	73	72	69	71	285	3816
Carin Hjalmarsson	71	72	71	74	288	3150
Marie Laure de Lorenzi	72	70	73	74	289	2191
Catherine Panton-Lewis	75	72	69	73	289	2191
Catrin Nilsmark	72	72	72	73	289	2191
Helen Wadsworth	71	70	69	79	289	2191

17-20 September
BMW ITALIAN OPEN
FRASANELLE GC, VENICE, ITALY

Laura Davies	66	66	73	69	274	£16500
Sandrine Mendiburu	74	70	65	70	279	11125
Corinne Dibnah	69	67	73	71	280	6820
Carin Hjalmarsson	70	72	68	70	280	6820
Sofia Gronberg	71	71	71	69	282	4664
Dale Reid	72	72	69	70	283	3850
Debbie Dowling	69	71	72	72	284	3300
Xonia Wunsch-Ruiz	71	69	72	73	285	2359
Leigh Ann Mills	70	69	72	74	285	2359
Li Wen-Lin	72	69	72	72	285	2359
Valerie Michaud	69	70	75	71	285	2359

24 - 27 September
THE 1992 WEETABIX BRITISH OPEN
WOBURN G & CC (DUKE'S COURSE)
MILTON KEYNES, ENGLAND

(See page 107)

9-11 October
SLOVENIAN OPEN
BLED GOLF & COUNTRY CLUB, SLOVENIA

Karen Lunn	71	70	141	£10500
Helen Hopkins	72	73	145	6002
Allison Shapcott	71	74	145	6002
Sara Robinson	70	76	146	3780
Rica Comstock	71	76	147	2317
Elena Girardi	78	69	147	2317
Catrin Nilsmark	72	75	147	2317
Lora Fairclough	73	74	147	2317
Lisa Hackney	72	76	148	1568

21-22 October
MOBIL CHALLENGE
EMIRATES GOLF CLUB, DUBAI

Dale Reid	74	68	142	£5000
Catherine Panton-Lewis	72	71	143	2500
Janice Arnold	71	73	144	1600
Federica Dassu	70	75	145	1300
Corinne Dibnah	73	74	147	1036
Gillian Stewart	73	74	147	1036
Lora Fairclough	72	75	147	1036
Carin Hjalmarsson	70	79	149	910
Helen Wadsworth	75	74	149	910

1992 · WPGE WINNERS SUMMARY

FORD LADIES' CLASSIC	Stefania Croce (Italy)
AGF LADIES' OPEN DE PARIS	Alison Nicholas (GB)
BMW EUROPEAN MASTERS	Kitrina Douglas (GB)
SKOL LA MANGA CLUB CLASSIC	Trish Johnson (GB)
THE EUROPEAN LADIES' OPEN	Laura Davies (GB)
HENNESSY LADIES' CUP	Helen Alfredsson (Swe)
LADIES' ENGLISH OPEN	Laura Davies (GB)
HOLIDAY INN LEIDEN LADIES' OPEN	Valerie Michaud (Fra)
IBM LADIES' OPEN	Helen Alfredsson (Swe)
BMW ITALIAN LADIES' OPEN	Laura Davies (GB)
WEETABIX WOMEN'S BRITISH OPEN	Patty Sheehan (USA)
SOLHEIM CUP	Europe
SLOVENIAN OPEN	Karen Lunn (Aus)
MOBIL CHALLENGE	Dale Reid GB

LEADING STROKE AVERAGES (VIVIEN SAUNDERS AWARD)

POS	PLAYER	ROUNDS	AVE
1	Laura Davies	34	70.35
2	Helen Alfredsson	19	70.37
3	Trish Johnson	35	71.51
4	Florence Descampe	19	71.58
5	Alison Nicholas	35	71.69
6	Suzanne Strudwick	37	72.08
7	Catrin Nilsmark	44	72.09
8	Corinne Dibnah	38	72.16
9	Alicia Dibos	31	72.39
10	Kristal Parker	29	72.62

Swedish rookie sensation Carin Hjalmarsson watches as Laura Davies storms to victory in the English Open at Tytherington

Ping Women's Golf Year

1992 · WPGE TOUR MONEY LIST: TOP 50

1	Laura Davies	£ 66,333	18	Valerie Michaud	18,441	34	Debbie Dowling	11,519
2	Helen Alfredsson	55,900	19	Allison Shapcott	17,879	35	Diane Barnard	11,368
3	Corinne Dibnah	53,212	20	Lisa Hackney	16,662	36	Helen Dobson	11,171
4	Trish Johnson	51,805	21	Janice Arnold	16,260	37	Xonia Wunsch-Ruiz	11,098
5	Catrin Nilsmark	35,728	22	Kristal Parker	16,058	38	Catherine Panton-Lewis	9,346
6	Marie Laure de Lorenzi	34,922	23	Lora Fairclough	15,770	39	Kathryn Marshall	9,277
7	Liselotte Neumann	34,202	24	Federica Dassu	14,493	40	Sara Robinson	8,311
8	Alison Nicholas	31,584	25	Sofia Gronberg	13,606	41	Li Wen-Lin	8,040
9	Kitrina Douglas	31,511	26	Laurette Maritz-Atkins	13,210	42	Malin Burstrom	7,890
10	Sandrine Mendiburu	26,896	27	Evelyn Orley	13,184	43	Susan Moon	7,662
11	Alicia Dibos	26,509	28	Corinne Soules	13,053	44	Kim Lasken	7,477
12	Stefania Croce	24,329	29	Jane Hill	12,656	45	Karine Espinasse	7,443
13	Suzanne Strudwick	24,043	30	Helen Wadsworth	12,606	46	Julie Forbes	7,436
14	Dale Reid	20,081	31	Leigh Ann Mills	12,176	47	Mardi Lunn	7,224
15	Carin Hjalmarsson	20,015	32	Gillian Stewart	11,906	48	Regine Lautens	7,099
16	Florence Descampe	19,425	33	Tania Abitbol	11,524	49	Claire Duffy	7,075
17	Karen Lunn	18,636				50	Nadene Hall	6,941

Ping Women's Golf Year

Laura Davies

EUROPEAN GOLFER OF THE YEAR

A Profile by Patricia Davies

There really was no doubt whatsoever about Europe's woman golfer of 1992. An incomparable performance in the Solheim Cup at Dalmahoy ended any argument, even from the Swedes who had a very valid claim to the title. Over three dank, dark days in Scotland in October, it became obvious to all: there's only one Laura Davies.

As the Europeans marmalised the Americans, widely regarded as unbeatable, by 11½ points to 6½, Davies was the home side's Seve-like inspiration. She won three matches out of three, starting the singles rout - 7-3 to Europe - by defeating Brandie Burton at the top of the order and underlining that she is the most charismatic and irresistible player in the world when the mood takes her.

Fortunately for her fellow competitors, the mood doesn't take her like that too often, for which Davies has a simple explanation: 'I'd be in the loony bin, wouldn't I?'

Davies, who was 29 the day after the Solheim Cup victory, is essentially an easy-going soul. She likes nothing better than being at home with her family and friends, sticking a salmon in the oven before setting off, not to practise but to shop, something she does nearly as well as she plays golf. The mall is one of the joys of her life in America, a shopper's paradise that could have been designed to fit in with a professional golfer's hours. Rita, Davies' mother, sighs indulgently as she awaits the results of yet another expedition.

For Davies, money is for spending, not just on herself but on everyone who means anything to her. She has a generous nature and, fortunately, a talent that allows her to make enough to indulge it almost to the full - there's no Ferrari in her mother's garage yet. Last year, she made £66,333 as the Number One in Europe and $150,163 in the United States, where she finished 39th on the money list. There was also an unspecified number of yen the result of various lucrative forays to Japan.

The Japanese, who are mad about golf in all its forms, have been mad about Davies since she stunned the golfing world, herself included, by winning the US Women's Open at Plainfield, New Jersey, in 1987. The action was followed even more avidly than usual in Japan because one of the players the tall, blonde Englishwoman beat in the 18-hole playoff for the title was Ayako Okamoto, a Japanese sporting icon. Small, dark and a neat, tidy hitter with a magical short game, Okamoto has her own television programme in Japan and her fulsome tributes to Davies - 'a player from another dimension' is a rough translation of one of her comments - helped ensure another star was born out east.

Moreover, she continued to do well out west. In 1988, Davies won twice in America

Laura Davies is the undisputed queen of European golf: (above) The Power; (right) The Glory

and was runner-up in the rookie of the year stakes, behind Liselotte Neumann, the Swede who followed Davies as US Open champion. Between them they set the standard for other Europeans to follow and paved the way for that remarkable Solheim Cup victory. Before the match, Beth Daniel reckoned that only Davies and Neumann would be of much use to the US side, afterwards the American was not available for comment - although to her credit she did hoick her golf bag into the European team room to have it signed.

It was the thoughtless arrogance of remarks like Daniel's (which neutral observers might have found hard to refute) that instilled in the Europeans the burning desire to prove that, underdogs or not, they could, nay would beat the Americans. Davies and her team-mates, especially those who played regularly in America, respected the quality of the opposition but knew from daily observation that they were not immortal, that they were fallible. Ever since the inaugural Solheim Cup match, at Lake Nona, in Florida, where the Americans won easily and everybody yawned ho-hum, Davies & Co had plotted their revenge.

There's no doubt that an incredible passion fuelled the result at Dalmahoy. 'They're not like this on Tour,' one of the American team said rather plaintively and her opponents were indeed like women possessed. Mickey Walker, the European captain, who was the women's Jacklin to Davies' Ballesteros, told a tale that confirmed as much. 'One of the days, at a team get-together, Laura said she'd spoken to her ball every time it was on the green and told it it was going in the hole. Someone laughed and Laura said, in all seriousness, ' No. It has no option'. She was

an inspiration.

'I really feel,' Walker said, 'that Laura was invincible that week. It didn't matter who she played or how well they played, she was always going to play well enough to win.'

This, mark you, was the woman who had played indifferently in the Weetabix Women's British Open at Woburn the week before, who had missed the cut in the US Open - her biggest disappointment of 1992 - and had missed four cuts in a row at the start of the season in America. However, these poor showings were more than offset by three victories in Europe and two near victories in the States where she lost out in playoffs, first to Anne-Marie Palli of France, then to the incomparable Nancy Lopez.

Davies, one of nature's gamblers, is still a touch unpredictable on the golf course but she is never dull - 'you can't make Laura Davies play conservatively,' Daniel once observed - but she is becoming more consistent. 'She's got an awful lot more control about her swing,' Walker said, 'and I think she's got a better understanding of the way it ticks, even though she has no desire to go into great depth on the theory.'

Although instinctively a hater of practice, Davies' growing maturity and professionalism now lead her to the practice ground more often than in the past and Mark Fulcher, who has taken over from her brother Tony as caddie, is trying to nudge her in that direction more often after a round. Having worked for the obsessive, and demanding Florence Descampe, Fulcher knows the sort of work other talented people put in and he does not want Davies, arguably the most talented of them all, to lose ground needlessly.

'She does practise a bit more,' confirmed

Tony, now his sister's manager, 'and everything's improved a little bit, although she still tends to play as she feels. It's little bits and pieces that have changed over the years but her temperament - that's the big change. She's a lot less liable to go off the deep end if things aren't going well. She's

advertisement of Tommy Lasorda, the baseball great she remembered as 'that fat Italian', looking slim and trim extolling the virtues of a slimming drink. La Davies, a sports nut, was suitably inspired and went on to lose

Although famed for her prodigious long-hitting, Davies also has a marvellous short game

definitely a lot calmer and handles things a lot better.'

Davies, who has the stubborn streak essential to all exceptional performers, is very much her own woman and does not like being told how to do things. She will absorb and assimilate advice in her own good time but shuns such modern golfing accoutrements as coaches, psychologists and fitness trainers. Having put on a lot of weight in 1991, however, she was prompted to lose it when she saw a television

upwards of three stones, a transformation that necessitated a complete change of wardrobe - no hardship for a fashion fiend and shopaholic. She intended losing another couple of stones in 1993.

The results could be frightening: with her all-round confidence boosted by a new not-so-round figure and yet another new wardrobe and her playing confidence sky-high, Laura Davies should have a ball. And so should the rest of us, just watching.

Amateur Golf in Europe

From Florida in January to Vancouver in late September, the amateur women golfers of Europe enjoyed a season of unprecedented success in 1992, and, from a Great Britain and Ireland stand point, the Curtis Cup triumph at Hoylake was quite simply the icing on the cake (as the Ladies' Golf

Estefania Knuth led Spain to victory in the Espirito Trophy

Union celebrates its centenary in 1993 we may as well plant 100 candles on the top for good measure).

The Curtis Cup (reviewed in chapter three) provided an exhibition of matchplay golf at its finest; almost as old as that competition is a prestigious American matchplay event, the Doherty Cup, which was first contested in 1933, one year after the inaugural Curtis Cup. In 1992, for the first time in its 59 year history, a non-American player won the trophy when Scotland's Catriona Lambert defeated Vicki Thomas of Wales in an all-British final at Coral Ridge, Fort Lauderdale, Florida.

The Doherty Cup has become part of a short winter amateur circuit in Florida known as the 'Orange Blossom Tour'. A second British victory on that tour nearly happened when 18-year-olds Nicola Buxton and Caroline Hall were defeated in a play-off for the Harder Hall Invitational by American Curtis Cup player, Carol Semple Thompson.

Back in Europe the most significant event at the beginning of the year was the Spanish Amateur Championship staged at the magnificent El Saler Course in March, and which saw Britain's Julie Hall defeat Italian Silvia Cavalleri in the final.

It certainly wasn't just the British players who were picking up the major silverware though, for the biggest amateur prize of all in Europe, the British Women's Amateur

Championship was won by Denmark's Pernille Pedersen, who thus became the first ever Scandinavian winner of that event (see overleaf). By contrast, the European Ladies Championship, which in 1992 was staged in Estoril, Portugal, produced a first ever British champion when Joanne Morley played four superbly consistent rounds of 71-72-72-69 to win by three strokes from Spain's Estafania Knuth and by five from a second Spanish player, Laura Navarro.

Morley was probably Britain's leading amateur player in 1992; in addition to her European Championship win she successfully defended her English Women's Strokeplay title at Littlestone, was the beaten finalist in the British Amateur and was undefeated in the Curtis Cup. Close behind Morley were Caroline Hall and Catriona Lambert (both of whom similarly impressed at Hoylake) and Joanne Hockley, who didn't make a debut in the Curtis Cup but did win the British Women's Strokeplay Championship at Frilford Heath and later teamed up with Morley and Lambert to represent Great Britain and Ireland in the World Amateur Team Championship (Espirito Trophy) in Vancouver. Heading the list of rising stars in the British amateur game are Lisa Walton, Janice Moodie and Mhairi McKay.

There are plenty of rising stars on the continent as well. The aforementioned World Amateur Team Championship, for so many years dominated by the United States, was claimed by Spain last September (see page 131), while the leading individual prize was won by Annika Sorenstam of Sweden.

As in 1991, Sorenstam played nearly all of her golf last year in America where, together with Vicki Goetze, she dominated the women's amateur scene. Sorenstam, like England's Caroline Hall, has since turned

professional; she will clearly be a great loss to the amateur game and it is a shame that Europeans have seen so little of her for she is undoubtedly an outstanding prospect. The

Joanne Morley was beaten in the final of last year's British Amateur at Saunton but later became the first British player to win the European Women's title

consolation is that when one Swedish prodigy passes into the professional ranks another always seems to be waiting somewhere in the wings.

British Women's Amateur Championship

The 1992 British Women's Amateur was staged at Saunton in the South West of England, just a week after the Curtis Cup. Saunton cannot pretend to boast the history and tradition of a Hoylake but as an examination of classic links type golf, with its natural humps and hollows, plateau greens and towering sand dunes, it has few equals.

A high class field - several Curtis Cup players from both sides were present - enjoyed the wonderful North Devon location and even some wonderful weather (a real contrast to Hoylake!) For the second week running Vicki Goetze led the American challenge, but was knocked out of the championship quite early in the week by Kristel D'Algue of France. The last surviving American, Carol Semple Thompson, reached the quarter-final stages before being beaten by Britain's Joanne Morley. The Cheshire player then progressed all the way to the final and it seemed likely that her opponent would be one of her Curtis Cup team-mates, Scotland's in-form Catriona Lambert.

Enter the 'Great Dane'. Pernille Pedersen had slipped, almost unnoticed, into the semi-finals. No Scandinavian player had ever won the championship and, prior to Saunton, the 27-year-old was probably best known as her country's former skiing champion. But she is undoubtedly a very fine golfer too, as Lambert and Morley discovered to their cost.

Both the semi-finals and final were played on the same day. As lunch-time approached an all-British contest for the afternoon looked probable with Morley having defeated Tracy Eakin 3 and 2 and Lambert one up on Pedersen with two to play; but the Danish player chose to rewrite the script and, with a little assistance from Lambert, contrived to win the last two holes.

In the final Morley got off to a poor start and found herself three down with eight holes to play. However, she managed to battle her way back to all-square by winning the 11th, 12th and 14th. On the par three 17th Morley looked set to go one up but the Danish player courageously holed a 15 footer for a half. With that timely putt Pedersen seized the initiative and went on to win the match at the final hole. And for the rest of that day at least, Devon belonged to Denmark.

June 10 - 14
1992 WOMEN'S AMATEUR CHAMPIONSHIP
SAUNTON, DEVON

QUARTER-FINALS:
P Pedersen (Denmark) beat L Walton 4 and 3
C Lambert beat K D'Algue (France) 4 and 3
T Eakin beat T Samuel (Canada) at 19th
J Morley beat C Semple Thompson (US) 1 hole

SEMI-FINALS:
P Pedersen beat C Lambert 1 hole
J.Morley beat T Eakin 3 and 2

FINAL
P PEDERSEN beat J MORLEY 1 hole

· ROLL OF HONOUR ·

1893	Lady Margaret Scott	1934	Helen Holm	1977	Angela Uzielli
1894	Lady Margaret Scott	1935	Wanda Morgan	1978	Edwina Kennedy (Aus)
1895	Lady Margaret Scott	1936	Pam Barton	1979	Maureen Madill
1896	Amy Pascoe	1937	Jessie Anderson	1980	Anne Quast Sander (USA)
1897	Edith O Orr	1938	Helen Holm	1981	Belle Robertson
1898	Miss L Thomson	1939	Pam Barton	1982	Kitrina Douglas
1899	May Hezlet	1940	No competition	1983	Jill Thornhill
1900	Rhona Adair	1941	No competition	1984	Jody Rosenthal (USA)
1901	Miss Graham	1942-5	No competition	1985	Lillian Behan (Ire)
1902	May Hezlet	1946	Jean Hetherington	1986	Marnie McGuire (NZ)
1903	Rhona Adair	1947	Babe Zaharias (USA)	1987	Janet Collingham
1904	Lottie Dod	1948	Louise Suggs (USA)	1988	Joanne Furby
1905	Miss B Thompson	1949	Frances Stephens	1989	Helen Dobson
1906	Mrs Kennion	1950	Vicomtesse de St Sauveur (Fr)	1990	Julie Hall
1907	May Hezlet	1951	Mrs P G MacCann	1991	Valerie Michaud (Fr)
1908	Miss M Titterton	1952	Moira Paterson	1992	Pernille Pedersen (Den)
1909	Dorothy Campbell	1953	Marlene Stewart (Can)		
1910	Grant Suttie	1954	Frances Stephens		
1911	Dorothy Campbell	1955	Jessie Anderson Valentine		
1912	Gladys Ravenscroft	1956	Margaret Smith		
1913	Muriel Dodd	1957	Philomena Garvey		
1914	Cecil Leitch	1958	Jessie Anderson Valentine		
1915	No competition	1959	Elizabeth Price		
1916	No competition	1960	Barabara McIntire (USA)		
1917-8	No competition	1961	Marley Spearman		
1919	No competition	1962	Marley Spearman		
1920	Cecil Leitch	1963	Brigitte Varangot (Fr)		
1921	Cecil Leitch	1964	Carol Sorenson (USA)		
1922	Joyce Wethered	1965	Brigitte Varangot (Fr)		
1923	Doris Chambers	1966	Elizabeth Chadwick		
1924	Joyce Wethered	1967	Elizabeth Chadwick		
1925	Joyce Wethered	1968	Brigitte Varangot (Fr)		
1926	Cecil Leitch	1969	Catherine Lacoste (Fr)		
1927	Thion de la Chaume (Fr)	1970	Dinah Oxley		
1928	Nanette Le Blan (Fr)	1971	Mickey Walker		
1929	Joyce Wethered	1972	Mickey Walker		
1930	Diana Fishwick	1973	Ann Irvin		
1931	Enid Wilson	1974	Carol Semple (USA)		
1932	Enid Wilson	1975	Nancy Syms (USA)		
1933	Enid Wilson	1976	Cathy Panton		

Denmark's Pernille Pedersen

Ping Women's Golf Year

6
The Rest of the World

Asia and Australia

Researched by Bill Johnson

S pain's Tania Abitbol lists music among her hobbies and she certainly called the tune when consistency earned her last year's Asian Order of Merit title after the five tournaments on the 1992 Kosaido Ladies' Asia Golf Circuit.

She finished ahead of Britain's Suzanne Strudwick with Alicia Dibos from Peru in third place. Abitbol crowned her five weeks in Asia with a convincing victory in the Singapore Open which was played over the Tanah Merah Country Club course.

The Spaniard was one of two European winners in Asia, the other **Li Wen-Lin** being Alison Nicholas, the

former British Open champion, who captured the Malaysian Open at Kelab Negara, Subang.

Japanese golfers also claimed two titles in Asia last year, the first victory coming from Yuka Irie in the Indonesian Open at the spectacularly situated Bali Handara Kosaido Country Club. On a testing course Irie fashioned a superb final round 67 for a five stroke winning margin. The following week Hitomi Notsu from Japan emulated Irie's success to win the Thailand Open at the Phuket Golf and Country Club.

In 1991 Li Wen-Lin from the Republic of China won three of the five events to head the Order of Merit and it was on the cards for her compatriot Ai-Yu Tu to do likewise when she won her national title at Chang Gung in Taipei in gale-force winds.

This was the opening event of the Asia circuit, but, as it transpired, the only event in which Tu played before beginning her assault on the Japanese LPGA Tour where she finished third on the Money List.

There were also four women's professional tournaments in Australia in 1992 - two in February and two in December. Both of the early events produced British victories, with Penny Grice-Whittaker winning in Queensland and Alison Nicholas in Perth. But in December Wendy Doolan and Jane Crafter raised the home flag with wins in Victoria and on the Gold Coast.

1992 · LADIES' ASIAN TOUR

16 - 18 January
REPUBLIC OF CHINA OPEN

Ai-Yu Tu (ROC)	71	75	72	218
Huang Yueh-Chin (ROC)	73	74	73	220
S Mendiburu (Fr)	73	77	72	222
M Lunn (AUS)	78	72	73	223
S Strudwick (GB)	71	76	76	223

23 - 25 January
SINGAPORE OPEN

T Abitbol (Sp)	72	72	73	217
S Ginter (US)	75	71	74	220
A Cain (US)	78	71	71	220
S Mendiburu (Fr)	77	73	72	222
A Ravaioli (US)	75	76	72	223
A H Read (US)	76	77	70	223

30 Jan - 1 Feb
MALAYSIAN OPEN

A Nicholas (GB)	71	71	70	212
S Strudwick (GB)	67	71	75	213
S Prosser (GB)	72	70	73	215
M Lunn (Aus)	69	70	76	215
D Baldwin (US)	75	71	70	216
K Cornelius (US)	72	72	72	216

6 - 8 February
INDONESIA OPEN

Y Irie (Jap)	74	70	67	211
S Kumagai (Jap)	74	74	68	216
L A Mills (US)	73	70	74	217
P Dunlap (US)	72	75	70	217
F Nagata (Jap)	73	73	72	218

13 - 15 February
THAILAND OPEN

H Notsu (Jap)	75	72	67	214
R Lautens (Swi)	76	72	71	219
S Gronberg (Swe)	74	75	71	220
A Dibos (Peru)	74	73	73	220
L Brown (US)	73	74	73	220

Spain's Tania Abitbol

1992 · ORDER OF MERIT : TOP 10

1.	T Abitbol (Sp)	275 pts
2.	S Strudwick (GB)	216
3.	A Dibos (Per)	215
4.	Y Irie (Jap)	212
5.	K Lasken (US)	203
6.	R Lautens (Swi)	190
7.	L A Mills (US)	185
8.	S Mendiburu (Fr)	176
9.	M Endo (Jap)	172
10.	M Lunn (Aus)	170

AUSTRALIA'S 1992 WINNERS

HISHIKI LADIES' QUEENSLAND OPEN:
Penny Grice-Whittaker

TAKANO YURI LADIES' OPEN:
Alison Nicholas

HEART HEALTH VICTORIAN OPEN:
Wendy Doolan

ALPINE AUSTRALIAN MASTERS:
Jane Crafter

Japanese Tour Review

By 'Duke' Ishikawa

In 1992 the Japanese LPGA Tour won - and then lost - the heart of Patti Rizzo. The winner of four (US) LPGA tournaments, Rizzo had elected to play a full season on the Japanese Tour and was doing extremely successfully, when in late October it all came to an abrupt end.

The reason for this was that the Japanese powers-that-be decided in their wisdom not to offer Rizzo fully exempt status for the 1993 season. At the time of the announcement Rizzo, a good Japanese speaker and close friend of Ayako Okamoto, had won three tournaments and was the leading money winner. Japanese Tour headquarters stated that the American would only be exempt with regard to the three events she had won. Disappointed and disillusioned, Rizzo left Japan before the end of the 1992 season.

It goes almost without saying that the aforementioned Okamoto was a dominant force on both the Japanese and American tours - she won twice in Japan last year - but the main beneficiary of Rizzo's sudden departure was 30-year-old Ikuyo Shiotani. She overtook Rizzo and finished the season as leading money winner. The former junior athletics star won only one event in 1992 but played consistently well throughout the year; indeed her end of season winnings total was a Japanese LPGA Tour record.

In recent years, Taiwanese golfers have excelled on the Japanese ladies' tour. The finest of these has undoubtedly been Ai-Yu Tu who learned her golf at the famous Tamusui links under the instruction of one of golf's great teachers, the late Chen. Tu, the Tour's leading money winner on no fewer than six occasions, won two tournaments in the spring and a third in October. Her fellow Taiwanese, Bie-Shyun Huang also won an event in May.

Last year, however, it was the turn of Korean golfers to make a significant impact. Ok-Kee Ku, a US Tour regular, captured the Japanese LPGA Championship, one of the Tour's two Majors championships, while Lee Hidemi won two tournaments and finished fifth on the money list.

The Tour's other major title, the National Women's Open produced a very popular winner in 38-year-old veteran, Atsuko Hikage who, following a year plagued by injury, enjoyed a great comeback season in 1992.

In addition to Rizzo's hat-trick of wins two other Americans triumphed in Japan last year, namely Patty Sheehan in the Spring, and Betsy King in the Fall, and there were 'rest of the world' victories for Jennifer Savil of Australia and Sweden's Helen Alfredsson.

Not withstanding the fracas over the Rizzo affair, 1992 ended on a romantic note with leading money-winner Shiotani announcing her engagement to her high school sweetheart.

1992 · JAPAN LPGA TOUR ·

TOURNAMENT WINNERS

Starts	Kumiko Hiyoshi
Daikin	Patty Sheehan
Skycourt	Haruyo Miyazawa
Saishun Kan	Ikayo Shiotani
Kiban	Lee Hidemi
Tohato	Ayako Okamoto
Yamaha Cup	Ai-Yu Tu
Yonex	Ai-Yu Tu
Nasu	Patti Rizzo
Tatokichi	Bie-Shyun Huang
Konika World Ladies	Yuko Moriguchi
Yakult	Jennifer Sevil
Bridgestone	Fusako Nagata
Toto	Akane Ohshiro
Mitsubishi	Mayami Hirase
Suntory	Reiko Kashiwado
Dunlop	Hiromi Takamura
Japan's National Open	Atsuko Hikage
Mizuno	Kari Harada
Toyo	Atsuko Hikage
Junon	Hiromi Hiragata
Stanley	Lee Hidemi
An Queens	Reiko Kashiwado
NEC	Mayumi Murai
Ito-en	Aki Nakano
KTV	Ayako Okamoto
Japan LPGA Championship	Ok-Hee Ku
Asahi	Michiko Okada
Miyagi TV	Akane Ohshiro
Tokai	Chieko Nishida
Takara	Patti Rizzo
Fujitsu	Patti Rizzo
Itsuki	Ai-Yu Tu
Mazda Japan	Betsy King
Itoki Classic	Helen Alfredsson
Elleair	Junko Yasui
Meiji Cup	Aki Nakano

American Patti Rizzo was just an argument away from heading the Japanese Order of Merit

ORDER OF MERIT: TOP 20

1	Ikuyo Shiotani	Yen 57,799,649
2	Patti Rizzo	56,901,325
3	Ai-Yu Tu	56,089,852
4	Junko Yasui	54,146,519
5	Lee Hidemi	50,770,791
6	Ayako Okamoto	50,640,000
7	Nayoko Yoshikawa	40,422,600
8	Mauri Murai	40,317,904
9	Michiko Hattori	39,905,632
10	Kamiko Hiyoshi	39,619,211
11	Bie-Shyun Huang	37,720,166
12	Aki Nakano	37,644,731
13	Akane Ohshiro	37,405,904
14	Fusako Nagata	36,796,718
15	Yuko Moriguchii	35,661,493
16	Jennifer Sevil	33,208,805
17	Hiromi Takamura	32,630,582
18	Kari Harada	32,146,456
19	Atsuko Hikage	31,648,258
20	Reiko Kashiwado	31,105,041

The Sunrise Cup · Women's World Team Championship

By Bill Johnson

Liselotte Neumann and Helen Alfredsson, unbeaten in Europe's staggering Solheim Cup victory only two weeks earlier, produced superb golf in appalling conditions to give Sweden a deserved title in the inaugural Sunrise Cup, the women's version of the World Cup, at the Sunrise Golf and Country Club in Taipei.

The Swedes came through when their 13-over-par combined aggregate of 445 left them two ahead of England's Laura Davies and Trish Johnson with Americans Meg Mallon and Jane Geddes third, six strokes further behind. Victory was worth $100,000 to the Swedish duo while Neumann and Johnson collected an extra $20,000 each when they shared the individual crown with three-over-par totals of 219.

In cold print such scoring may appear to be high but it was genuinely magnificent in the conditions. Neumann and Alfredsson had to overcome both the superb Robert Trent Jones Jnr. designed course and Typhoon Yvette which was blowing in from the Philippines.

Practice rounds and the pro-am had to be cut short, then, on the opening day, the first round of the tournament was brought to an end by lashing rain and low cloud before any of the eight fourballs could complete the course. When play came to a halt Davies and Johnson from England, one over par after nine holes, led by a stroke from the Scottish team of Dale Reid and Pam Wright while Peru (Jenny Lidback and Alicia Dibos), Canada (Dawn Coe and Lisa Walters) and Sweden shared third place at four over.

The interruption meant that the players had to leave their Taipei hotel as early as 5.30am the next morning in order to complete the remaining holes before tackling the second round of the 54 holes tournament. Johnson (71) and Davies (74) put England ahead when the delayed round was finally completed. They still led by one stroke from Sweden's Neumann (71) and Alfredsson (75). Scotland, the United States and France (Marie-Laure de Lorenzi and Sandrine Mendiburu) were all five strokes off the pace.

When the second round started at around lunch time the wind became so ferocious that David Rollo, the tournament director, seriously considered suspending play but on they went. There were not surprisingly many tales of woe as the conditions took their toll during the long afternoon.

Yet no matter how difficult it becomes it seems there is always one player who is able to master the elements and on this occasion it was Neumann, who handed in an astonishing round of 70. Her partner Alfredsson managed a 76 which left Sweden on 292 and enabled them to move three clear of England for whom Johnson came in with a battling 72 and Davies a 78. Johnson had been three under after 14 holes but dropped shots at three of her last four holes while Davies had a seven at the 15th.

There was no respite on the final day when the wind was even stronger. Flag sticks were bent by the sheer strength of the wind. Greenkeepers not only had to replace

putts, three of these from less than a yard but England only gained one stroke. This was the first of a succession of near disasters as strokes disappeared like confetti in the wind. It all added up to Sweden being three ahead of England when they reached the downhill 471 yard par five 18th hole.

Sweden's
Lotte Neumann

flagsticks but were constantly repairing the damaged holes which had lost their shape.

Alfredsson stood firm at the outset and was one under par after the opening six holes. Neumann, Davies and Johnson were all three over for the same stretch. When Johnson dropped another shot at the 8th Sweden had advanced seven strokes clear of England, who indeed had now been overtaken by the Americans. But the 10th, a right hand dog-leg around a lake effectively extinguished American hopes as Geddes and Mallon both ran up double-bogey sixes. At the same hole Johnson made a second consecutive birdie for England to move four strokes clear of the Americans.

Sweden at this stage were six ahead of England as the tension increased and nerves began to fray. At the long 13th Neumann, her ball oscillating in the wind, took four

Davies produced an enormous drive then, directly into the teeth of the wind, she reached for her driver again and unbelievably found the green in two. Neumann had found sand with her tee shot while Alfredsson bunkered her approach. Neumann, still 25 yards from the hole, like Johnson, found the green in three but her partner was still short of the green after her recovery from sand. Were the Swedes going to be caught after all by England in what was becoming a thrilling climax?

It needed something special and Alfredsson rose to the occasion admirably. She chipped up from short of the green to eight feet from where she holed to match Johnson's par. Davies made her birdie but the final flourish came from Neumann who got down in two putts from 25 yards to seal a narrow victory for Sweden.

SUNRISE CUP · WOMEN'S WORLD TEAM CHAMPIONSHIP
16 - 18 OCTOBER 1992 · SUNRISE GOLF AND COUNTRY CLUB, TAIPEI, TAIWAN

Sweden **445**
L Neumann 71 70 78 219
H Alfredsson 75 76 75 226
$50,000 each

England **447**
T Johnson 71 72 76 219
L Davies 74 78 76 228
$35,000 each

USA **453**
J Geddes 74 72 76 222
M Mallon 77 76 78 231
$25,000 each

Switzerland **454**
E Orley 74 74 73 221
R Lautens 78 77 78 233
$20,000 each

Spain **456**
M Figueras-Dotti 72 73 77 222
T Abitbol 82 73 79 234
$15,000 each

Canada **459**
D Coe 75 75 78 228
L Walters 77 75 79 231
$11,000 each

Australia **459**
J Stephenson 75 71 77 223
C Dibnah 79 74 83 236
$11,000 each

Scotland **462**
D Reid 73 76 78 227
P Wright 78 76 81 235
$9,000 each

Wales **464**
K Davies 77 79 76 232
H Wadsworth 76 76 80 232
$8,000 each

Peru **465**
J Lidback 75 77 79 231
A Dibos 76 79 79 234
$7,000 each

France **470**
M L de Lorenzi 73 79 75 227
S Mendiburu 78 84 81 243
$6,500 each

Japan **474**
Y Irie 76 75 81 232
Y Kawanami 77 81 84 242
$6,000 each

South Africa **477**
L Maritz 82 76 76 234
A Sheard 82 82 79 243
$5,500 each

Republic of China **477**
Li Wen-Lin 79 81 72 232
Wang Mei-Yun 82 80 83 245
$5,500 each

Italy **477**
F Dassu 78 74 82 234
E Girardi 77 80 86 243
$5,500 each

South Korea **497**
Ko Woo Soon 80 77 89 246
Park Sung Ja 82 85 84 251
$5,000 each

Trish Johnson of England

LEADING INDIVIDUAL SCORES

T Johnson	71	72	76	219
L Neumann	71	70	78	219
E Orley	74	74	73	221
M Figueras-Dotti	72	73	77	222
J Geddes	74	72	76	222
J Stephenson	75	71	77	223
H Alfredsson	75	76	75	226
M L de Lorenzi	73	79	75	227
D Reid	73	76	78	227
L Davies	74	78	76	228
D Coe	75	75	78	228

Ping Women's Golf Year

The World Amateur Team Championship

24-27 SEPTEMBER 1992 • (FOR THE ESPIRITO SANTO TROPHY) VANCOUVER, CANADA

LEADING TEAM SCORES

Spain	588				
Macarena Campomanes	77	79	74	74	304
Estefania Knuth	74	73	73	72	292
Laura Navarro	80	71	74	78	303
Great Britain and Ireland	**589**				
Joanne Hockley	83	80	83	73	319
Joanne Morley	75	74	75	77	301
Catriona Lambert	70	73	76	73	292
New Zealand	**597**				
Lisa Aldridge	75	72	78	80	305
Lynette Brooky	74	73	76	78	301
Susan Farron	83	78	73	76	310
Sweden	**599**				
Linda Ericsson	78	77	82	86	323
Maria Hjorth	76	79	80	79	314
Annika Sorenstam	75	68	74	70	287
United States of America	**600**				
Vicki Goetze	78	71	74	76	299
Sarah Le Brun Ingram	80	79	76	78	313
Carol Semple Thompson	74	75	75	77	301

LEADING INDIVIDUAL SCORES

Annika Sorenstam (SWEDEN)	75	68	74	70	287
Estefania Knuth (SPAIN)	74	73	73	72	292
Catriona Lambert (GB & I)	70	73	76	73	292
Vicki Goetze (USA)	78	71	74	76	299
Ericka Jayatilaka (AUSTRALIA)	74	73	75	77	299
Delphine Bourson (FRANCE)	72	74	77	77	300
Chae Eun Song (KOREA)	75	74	76	75	300
Lynette Brooky (NZ)	74	73	76	78	301
Joanne Morley (GB & I)	75	74	75	77	301
Carol Semple Thompson (USA)	74	75	75	77	301
Yu-Cheng Huang (TAIPEI)	77	75	75	75	302
Caterin Quintarelli (ITALY)	73	74	73	82	302

• ROLL OF HONOUR •

YEAR	VENUE	WINNER	
1964	St Germain, France	France	588
1966	Mexico City CC	Unites States	580
1968	Victoria GC, Australia	United States	616
1970	Club de Campo, Spain	United States	598
1972	Hindu CC, Argentina	United States	583
1974	Campo de Golf, Dominica	United States	620
1976	Vilamoura, Portugal	United States	605
1978	Pacific Harbour, Fiji	Australia	596
1980	Pinehurst No 2, USA	United States	588
1982	Geneva, Switzerland	United States	579
1984	Royal Hong Kong	United States	585
1986	Caracas, Venezuela	Spain	580
1988	Drottingholm, Sweden	United States	587
1990	Christchurch, New Zealand	United States	585
1992	Vancouver, Canada	Spain	588

Annika Sorenstam

1993
An Eventful Season

7

Major Players,
Major Stages

From out of the shadows came Alfie
the Great... Helen Alfredsson's emergence
as a genuine world class player was
undoubtedly one of the highlights of 1992.
Who will similarly dazzle in 1993?
There is no Solheim or Curtis Cup this year,
but certainly no shortage of important
events, both professional and amateur.

In America, the four Majors will provide
the focus to an LPGA season that promises
much - especially as the Tour is developing
an increasingly international image.
Will Dottie dominate again? And how can
the 48th US Open at Crooked Stick surpass
last year's great spectacle at Oakmont?

In Europe, will the likes of Catrin
Nilsmark, Annika Sorenstam and Sandrine
Mendiburu threaten Laura Davies' number
one position? Which players will star in
Japan and Asia? And who will impress on
the amateur scene this summer?

The following pages outline some of
the leading events and personalities that
are likely to make 1993 another
memorable season.

January

Tanah Merah, Singapore: just as golf 'takes us to so many wonderful places' it also presents an array of mischievously positioned greens.

Golf is booming in South East Asia no less than it is in North America and Europe, and with the major women's professional tours not fully underway, the region is the main focus of championship golf early in the year. The Ladies' Asian Tour begins its five week circuit in Thailand and then heads south to Indonesia. In 1993 however, the WPG European Tour is also staging an event in this part of the world, the KRP World Ladies' Classic in Malaysia. Elsewhere, there are tournaments in Australia and several big amateur events in Florida.

February

The 1993 LPGA Tour commences in February and Dottie Mochrie begins the defence of her numerous titles and awards.

Two LPGA tournaments are scheduled for February, the Palm Beach Classic in Florida and the Itoki Hawaiian Open on the island of Oahu: Colleen Walker, who won three times in 1992, defends the former and Lisa Walters the latter. Walter's win last season triggered a hatrick of first time victories for Canadian players and her close friend Dawn Coe won the Kemper Open just seven days later. On the Asian Tour a great mix of nationalities will contest the Singapore and Malaysian Opens and then comes the circuit's final event, the Republic of China Open.

March

Photographers' delight – golfers' nightmare:
the splendid oasis-like setting of the Moon Valley Country Club
in Phoenix, Arizona.

Moon Valley hosts the Standard Register PING tournament in the third week of March, and Danielle Ammaccapane will be hoping for a third win in as many years. A strong field always assembles (in one recent year each of the top 100 players from the previous season's Money List competed); and none will want to miss the following event either - the first Major of 1993, the Nabisco Dinah Shore. Dottie Mochrie will be defending at Mission Hills, and earlier in the month, Brandie Burton defends her PING/Welch's title in Tucson.

April

Do you get the feeling that the gallery's behind her?
Stefania Croce leads the charge during last year's
Ford Classic at Woburn.

The Ford Golf Classic is the first of two WPG European Tour events that are to be staged at Woburn in 1993, the other, of course, being the Weetabix British Open in August. Ford's event is always held over the Duchess' Course whereas the Duke's Course hosts the Weetabix British Open. Magnificent pine trees border the fairways of both courses. The richest event on the LPGA Tour is also staged at the end of April (another Danielle Ammaccapane defence) and there are also LPGA tournaments in April at Las Vegas and Atlanta.

May

Twice beaten in Major championship playoffs last year, no player will be more determined or better prepared in 1993 than Juli Inkster.

The states of Tennessee, Delaware, Pennsylvania and New York host LPGA events in May; more specifically the Sara Lee Classic, McDonalds, Lady Keystone Open and Corning Classic tournaments. Of these the biggest prize is on offer at the McDonalds Championship at the Du Pont Country Club. The title is due to be defended by Japan's Ayako Okamoto; back in her native country, the Japanese LPGA Tour is in full flow come May, and the WPGE Tour visits The Hague in Holland for the Holiday Inn Leiden Open, won by France's Valerie Michaud in 1992.

June

A million grains of sand and one
golf ball; Kitrina Douglas executes a bunker shot
at the BMW European Masters.

Kitrina Douglas won the 1992 BMW European Masters at the Golf du Bercuit and the tournament returns to the Brussels venue again at the end of the month. There were a few raised eyebrows when the WPGE Tour announced its intention to stage an event in Slovenia last year, but the October event proved to be a success and a second Slovenian Open will be played a week before the European Masters. June is an important month for amateur golf with the British Ladies' Championship being staged at Royal Lytham and St Annes, while in America, Betsy King defends her Mazda LPGA Championship at Bethesda - and there will surely be no 11 stroke victory this time.

July

All calm at Crooked Stick; but it won't be
so in July this year when the US Women's Open
comes to Carmel, Indiana.

Crooked Stick is where the world first discovered 'Long John' Daly when the brash American smashed his way to victory in the 1991 US PGA Championship. If Crooked Stick maintains its reputation as a big-hitter's course then among golfers to watch for at the 48th US Women's Open in July will be Britain's Laura Davies (the winner in 1987) and Americans Brandie Burton and Michelle McGann. Two of the more important events on the 1993 WPGE Tour calendar take place in July, namely the European Open and the Hennessy Cup, and in the amateur game, Italy hosts the European Women's Championship.

August

Vast crowds are sure to flock to Woburn in August when American Patty Sheehan defends her Weetabix Women's British Open title.

It will not be a major upset if Patty succeeds again at Woburn (although it will be a marvellous achievement, for the entire cast of the WPGE Tour will be out to stop her), but it will be an amazing story if, two weeks later, Sherri Steinhauer repeats her 1992 du Maurier triumph - the Major championship victory in Winnipeg last year being the first LPGA win of her career. August is also likely to see Florence Descampe defending her first LPGA success at Stratton Mountain, and, at Chula Vista near San Diego, the nation's best amateurs will be competing for the US Amateur crown.

September

An English summer golfscape: green grass, blue skies and Laura Davies at Tytherington during last year's English Open championship.

Laura Davies played some sparkling golf to win the 1992 English Open by seven shots and if she returns to Tytherington this September she will almost certainly be the person to beat. The Cheshire course traditionally favours powerful hitters and for most players it represents a stern challenge (having said that, it was brought to its knees in the third round last year by Sweden's Carin Hjalmarsson who shot an incredible 64!) On the LPGA Tour, the PING - Cellular One tournament takes place in the middle of the month followed by the Safeco Classic - Nancy Lopez and Colleen Walker are the defending champions.

October

*Meet the 'raining' champions of Europe
and the reigning 'champions of the world' – Sweden's
Helen Alfredsson and Liselotte Neumann.*

The rain that brought out the umbrellas and the rain gear in the above picture was the same rain that brought smiles, not just to the two Swedes, but to the entire European team at Dalmahoy last October. Even heavier rain fell a fortnight later in the Sunrise (!) World Team Cup in Taiwan, but again there were Swedish celebrations as Alfredsson and Neumann finished ahead of the field. At the time of writing, no date (or venue) had been fixed for a 2nd World Cup, but at the end of the month an LPGA team will face a Japanese LPGA team in the annual Nichirei International.

LPGA Tour Schedule 1993

FEBRUARY

5-7   Palm Beach LPGA Classic, Wycliffe G & CC, Lake Worth, Fla.

18-20   Itoki Hawaiian Ladies Open, Ko Olina GC, Ewa Beach, Oahu, Haw.

MARCH

11-14   PING/Welch's Championship, Randolph Park North GC, Tucson, Ariz.

18-21   Standard Register PING, Moon Valley, Phoenix, Ariz.

25-28   Nabisco Dinah Shore*, Mission Hills CC, Rancho Mirage, Calif.

APRIL

2-4   Las Vegas LPGA at Canyon Gate, Canyon Gate CC, Las Vegas, Nev.

15-18   Atlanta Women's Championship, Eagle's Landing CC, Stockbridge, Ga.

29-2 May   Centel Classic, Killearn CC, Tallahassee, Fla.

MAY

7-9   Sara Lee Classic, Hermitage GC, Old Hickory, Tenn.

13-16   McDonald's Championship, Du Pont CC, Wilmington, Del.

21-23   Lady Keystone Open, Hershey CC, Hershey, Penn.

27-30   LPGA Corning Classic, Corning CC, Corning, NY.

29-30   JCPenney/LPGA Skins Game, Stonebriar CC, Frisco, Tex.

JUNE

3-6   Oldsmobile Classic, Walnut Hills CC, East Lansing, Mich.

10-13   Mazda LPGA Championship*, Bethesda CC, Bethesda, Md.

17-20   Rochester International, Locust Hill CC, Pittsford, NY.

25-27   ShopRite LPGA Classic, Greate Bay Resort & CC, Somers Point, N.J.

JULY

2-4   Jamie Farr Toledo Classic, Highland Meadows GC, Sylvania, Ohio

9-11   Youngstown-Warren LPGA Classic, Avalon Lakes, Warren, Ohio

15-18   JAL Big Apple Classic, Wykagyl CC, New Rochelle, N.Y.

22-25   US Women's Open*, Crooked Stick GC, Carmel, Ind.

29-1 Aug   PING/Welch's Championship, Blue Hill CC, Canton, Mass.

AUGUST

5-8   McCall's LPGA Classic at Stratton Mountain, Stratton Mountain CC, Stratton Mountain, Ver.

12-15   Sun-Times Challenge, White Eagle GC, Naperville, Ill.

20-22   Minnesota LPGA Classic, Edinburgh USA GC, Brooklyn Park, Minn.

26-29   Du Maurier Ltd. Classic*, London H&CC, London, Ont., Canada

SEPTEMBER

4-6   State Farm Rail Classic, Rail GC, Springfield, Ill.

10-12   PING-Cellular One LPGA Golf Championship, Columbia Edgewater CC, Portland, Ore.

16-19   Safeco Classic, Meridian Valley CC, Kent, Wash.

23-25   Kyocera Inamori Classic, TBA

30-3 Oct   Los Coyotes LPGA Classic, Los Coyotes CC, Buena Park, Calif.

OCTOBER

15-17   World Championship of Women's Golf, TBA

29-31   Nichirei International, Japan

NOVEMBER

5-7   The Japan Classic, TBA

DECEMBER

2-5   JCPenney Classic, Innisbrook Resort, Tarpon Springs, Fla.

9-12   LPGA Match Play Championship, Beach Course, Waikoloa, Haw.

25-26   Wendy's Three-Tour Challenge, New Albany CC, Columbus, Ohio

* Major Championship • TBA To Be Arranged